The Miracle of the Kurds

Also by Stephen Mansfield

The Character and Greatness of Winston Churchill:
Hero in a Time of Crisis

Then Darkness Fled:
The Liberating Wisdom of Booker T. Washington

Forgotten Founding Father:
The Heroic Legacy of George Whitefield

The Faith of George W. Bush

The Faith of the American Soldier

Pope Benedict XVI: His Life and Mission

The Faith of Barack Obama

The Search for God and Guinness

Lincoln's Battle with God

Killing Jesus

Mansfield's Book of Manly Men

THE MIRACLE OF THE KURDS

A Remarkable Story of Hope
Reborn in Northern Iraq

STEPHEN MANSFIELD

WORTHY®
PUBLISHING

Published by Worthy Publishing, a division of Worthy Media, Inc., 134 Franklin Road, Suite 200, Brentwood, Tennessee 37027.

WORTHY is a registered trademark of Worthy Media, Inc.

eBook available wherever digital books are sold.

Library of Congress Control Number: 2014944654

Cover Design: Christopher Tobias, Tobias' Outerwear for Books
Author Photo: Isaac Darnall
Cover Photo of people: © Magnum Photos
Cover Photo of Grand Millennium Sulaimani Hotel: Sabah Mustafa Muhammed
        © 2014 The Mansfield Group
Interior Design and Typesetting: Christopher D. Hudson & Associates, Inc.

For foreign and subsidiary rights, contact rights@worthypublishing.com

ISBN: 978-1-61795-079-7 (hardcover w/ jacket)

To Noor, Farrah & Mejid

I will always hold your stories in my heart.

CONTENTS

From this day on

She was a flute,

And the hand of the wind

Endowed her wounds with melodies

She has been singing ever since for the world.

—Kurdish Poet Sherko Bekas,
writing of Kurdistan

AN AUTHOR'S DEBT

There is a great debt I have incurred during the years that have formed themselves into this book and it is to the Kurdish people themselves. It is the debt I owe them for changing my life.

When I first began to travel among the Kurds of Kurdistan in the early 1990s, it was as part of an international relief team. I confess the experience impressed me almost entirely as a grand adventure. I had never been in the Middle East before. To fly from the United States to Istanbul and then on to Diyarbakir in eastern Turkey before driving five hours south to Duhok, Iraq, seemed the exotic expedition of a lifetime.

In those days, Turkish troops patrolled the roads into Kurdistan. We were stopped often. Machine gun fire echoed in the distance and our vehicles wove warily around tanks strategically positioned on mountain roads. We ate in roadside villages so old and so fixed at the heart of the

Fertile Crescent that the patriarch Abraham might well have dined in the same villages millennia before.

It was, I confess with regret, the journey itself that initially thrilled me most. My exaggerated sense of adventure was further inflated when the Turks closed the roads into northern Iraq. This forced our team to fly into Damascus before making a nine-hour drive across the Syrian Desert.

I thus found myself in what I ignorantly thought of as Arabia. It was intoxicating. Images from the writings of T. E. Lawrence—"Lawrence of Arabia"—played in my mind. Bedouin men stared at us curiously from their easy perches atop unruly camels. Black tents dotted the eternal sands and seemed in their undulations to breathe for that great living being, the desert. I touched the ancient stones at Palmyra, ate fresh *naan*—the round flat bread of the Middle East—by open fires, and dragged my fingers in the waters of the Euphrates when, finally, an unsteady motorboat carried our team to the far shore of Kurdistan.

I am ashamed that the journey ever meant more to me than the people, but for a season it did. I put this down to the myopia of youth and to the overly domesticated life I was living at the time. Thankfully, when the greater meaning of my experience announced itself, it came white hot and impatient, searing itself permanently into my soul.

This happened as Kurds lovingly took me by the hand and pulled me into their world. I soon found myself in touch with something vital and ageless. So enriching and ancient were the lessons the Kurds had to teach, it often made my life in the West seem thin and meaningless. Mysteriously, the impartation from each experience among my new friends was much greater than the experience itself. Perhaps this is the way of all liturgies. The land, the embrace of a generous yet fierce people, the nobility of tribe and custom, and the always-audible echo of the Kurdish sufferings each mystically became part of me. So began a transformation—of manhood, of honor, of my understanding of history, of the way I viewed my life in this world—that continues to this moment.

Many faithful friends have contributed liberally to this book. I acknowledge most of them toward the end of these pages. I trust none of them will be offended if I offer but one expression of gratitude here at the beginning. It is this: I owe a great debt—one I cannot repay—to the Kurds I have known around the world. Thank you, my dear friends, for refusing to leave me as I was.

—Stephen Mansfield

A Word on Literary Liberties

The story of the Kurds presented in this book is true, as is each event described in these pages. The author has used pseudonyms if requested or if security required. In addition, the author has conflated some stories for clarity.

CHAPTER 1

OF KURDS, CURSES, AND JAM

"In the area of Iraq that was liberated from Saddam Hussein's control the earliest—the Kurdish provinces in the northeast part of the country—all objective observers seem to agree that an unprecedented prosperity has replaced what was once an unimaginable wasteland of misery. With their head-start of liberation beginning in 1992, the Kurds have nonetheless set an example for the rest of the region as well as of the country."

—Christopher Hitchens[1]

We have jam. But we have no jam." I smiled when I heard these words. I had heard them before. I had not expected to hear them aboard a Royal Jordanian jet flying high above the Syrian Desert.

1

Perhaps I had not heard them at all. It was that artificial morning that comes after a long overnight flight eastward from the United States. I had just awakened and was disoriented. Moments before, flight attendants had cheerily urged passengers to greet the new day by opening their window shades. It was an evil suggestion. Lasers of light shot through the dark cabin. I shielded my eyes against this assault and tried to locate the face that belonged to those familiar words.

Slowly, I pieced the previous moments together in my mind. Breakfast was being served. The British gentleman next to me, having already eaten all the jam willingly surrendered by passengers nearby, went in search of more. He inquired of a flight attendant. This is what occasioned that memorable sentence. "We have jam," the woman said in the stoic civility of her profession, "but we have no jam." The words were a subtle study in metaphysics. *Jam exists in the universe,* she was saying, *but it does not exist on this flight.*

While my British friend grumbled his displeasure, I thought back to the first time I had heard the unusual phrases. It was nearly twenty years before. I remember that I was asked to speak at a conference in the Iraqi city of Erbil. In those days, both Iraq and the Kurds who populated Erbil were in a tense season, pressed as they were between wars, between alliances and between competing visions of Kurdish destiny.

It was the early 1990s. The Persian Gulf War had ended only a few years before. A civil war had since erupted between the two dominant Kurdish political parties. To nearly everyone's surprise, Saddam Hussein still threat-ened from the south, the Coalition of nations that drove him from Kuwait having chosen not to drive him from power. Then there was the grief that hung thickly over northern Iraq—the Kurds prefer the name *Kurdistan*—from the loss of tens of thousands of lives. Many of these were victims of chemical weapons. Others were shot, starved, landmined, or tortured to death. Nearly all were Kurdish victims of the Iraqi regime of Saddam Hussein.

In the Erbil of that turbulent time, I joined my fellow conference leaders at our hotel restaurant for breakfast one morning. During the laborious process of ordering food through bits and pieces of an unfamiliar language, a friend asked our waiter if there was jam. "We have jam," the man said brightly, eyebrows raised and teeth gleaming beneath an impeccably trimmed moustache, eager to confirm the sweet luxury existed in his land. "But we have no jam." These last words were said with an almost mock expression of sadness, as though to assure my fellow teacher that all who knew the glories of jam—Kurdish jam-lovers in particular—shared his disappointment.

I remember that we were grateful for the waiter's quick disappearance into the kitchen. We would not have offended

3

for the world, but we could not have held our laughter much longer given the contradictory words and the practiced way the waiter said them.

We have jam, but there is no jam. Jam exists, but it does not exist here. The spirit of jam is with us, but not the incarnation.

For the remainder of that breakfast, we enjoyed trying out humorous variations of those words. It was all great fun and it continued as the story of the waiter's single sentence was recounted over the following days. It was good for a laugh but soon something more began to emerge. With each retelling, the waiter's words seemed to take on a broader meaning. They quickly became a type of shorthand for the unfortunate truth that the world often disappoints, that the promise and the reality of life are frequently two very different things. If the lights went out during a lecture— as they regularly did in those days—someone was sure to shout from the dark, "We have jam, but we have no jam." An explosion of laughter would follow. Heads would nod as though in agreement with some inside knowledge denied to the outer world. It was the same if the hotel ran out of hot water or if some security threat proved an inconvenience. In the larger gatherings, the words became a humorous liturgy of discontent. "We have jam," those sitting on one side of the room would offer. "But we have no jam," came the rejoinder from the other side. And so it went for days.

In time, the waiter's seemingly insignificant phrases took on harsher meaning. They began to invoke all the aching realities of the Kurds—the ironies of Kurdish life, the betrayals and tragedies that marked the Kurdish place in the world. It was as though the whole of the Kurdish plight distilled into those eight words. *We have jam, but we have no jam.* This is because *we are a people, but we are no people. We are a nation, but we have no nation. We have friends, but, in truth, we have no friends at all in the world.*

The words began to sting. From their innocent first mention at that breakfast, they were redeployed into a euphemism for the whole of the curse history has flung upon the Kurds. I knew this was true when on the last day of the conference someone used the familiar sentence once again. There were weary, forced grunts of laughter. It was all getting a bit old. Yet I happened to glance at an American friend just then and I saw the tears forming in his eyes. This new meaning had become too much for him, loving the Kurds as he did. He could no longer stoically endure the tension between what existed in the world and what existed for the Kurds in those days. He was grieved for a people who knew there was jam in the world but who never seemed to have any of their own.

Remembering the origins of "the jam story" caused me to recall, too, the dangerous, war-ravaged place that Kurdistan was in the early 1990s.

To be among the Kurds in the northern Iraq of those days was to be in the middle of a civil war while the troops of a tyrant amassed on a nearby border. Economic sanctions added to the general miseries by making life disease-ridden and spare. Makeshift checkpoints punctuated cratered roads. So quickly could fighting erupt that men carried their Kalashnikov machine guns while strolling markets with their families. Grocery stores were seldom more than shelf-lined half-huts partially rebuilt from loose stones and rubble. Streets were muddy and crowded. The sound of explosions nearby cleared them instantly. Jets and helicopters flew deafeningly overhead while those on the ground prayed Saddam Hussein had not sent them.

Tragedies mounted upon the Kurds. Medicines were difficult to obtain and diseases were often left to run their devastating course. Landmines dotted the landscape, particularly in those areas where Kurds grew food. This was a gift of the Iraqi regime. Stories circulated about flocks of sheep wandering harmlessly over mines that were then triggered by the shepherds who followed behind. Limbs were lost, as were lives. Survival became, in part, about detecting threats by sound alone. There were the low, rumbling sounds of heavier weapons echoing from the hills or some plain far away. These signaled little threat. Still, it was wise to listen for changes. It was also wise to listen carefully to the light machine gun fire that sometimes pierced the night from nearby neighborhoods. It was wise to listen, but there was little to be done about it except to pray against ricochets and try to sleep.

The tension was suffocating. The Asaish, the Kurdish secret police, were understandably ever-present. During one idle afternoon in an Erbil hotel, I decided to stick my video camera out the window to film some of the landscape. Despite the fact that I was on the seventh floor and it was a cloudy day, a squad of Asaish appeared at my door within minutes to ask whom I was working for. I tried to explain, with the help of my interpreter, that I was working for two children back home who were eager to understand what Daddy was doing in Iraq. The Asaish weren't having it. They confiscated my film cartridges and told me to restrict my picture taking to the restaurant.

This ever-present tension could give way to extreme danger without warning. One of the worst of our experiences occurred as we were attempting to cross the border from Turkey into Kurdistan late one afternoon. As the sun was starting to set and we were submitting our papers to border guards, a unit of Kurdish PKK guerrillas began shooting at the Turks. Tracer fire sizzled through the air in great arcs of light. Machine guns answered from sandbagged positions. Idiot that I am, I stood to watch it all until one of the men on our team shouted me to the ground. It was all over in seconds.

Fearing a second attack, the Turks decided to close the border. We found ourselves, then, effectively locked out of Kurdistan and forced to spend the night in a region that made me think of the Old American West supplied with machine guns and rocket-propelled grenades (RPGs). We found rooms in a seedy, war-ravaged town called Silopi. Sleep came in short bursts, kept at bay by soldiers creeping warily through the streets, periodic exchanges of gunfire, and—sometimes far worse—silence.

It was just this intermittent nature of danger that could prove deadly. Because Kurdistan was embroiled in a guerrilla war rather than a "hot war," it was easy to forget where you were. On one occasion, our team met at length with Kurdish officials in a mountaintop complex. The floor-to-ceiling windows of the conference room revealed stunning scenery. I had lived near the Alps in my youth but had never seen such drama of snow and stone. Weary and yet transfixed by the view, I could barely concentrate on the business before us. I sipped tea and relaxed on a leather divan while other team members pressed a case of one kind or another. I had drifted far away, peaceful and unknowing, when a U.S. F-16 fighter jet roared into view and began circling. So violent were the percussions from the jet's engines that windows rattled and tea sloshed in cups. The wings were turned so steeply and the pilot flew so near that it was as though he was leaning in at high speed to catch bits of our conversation. I was thrust back to the realities of time and space: "I am in a war zone. I am kept alive mainly by an invisible thing called a no-fly zone. Try to pay attention, Stephen."

That was all, as I've said, in the early 1990s. Two decades later, I pulled my thoughts from jam and Kurdish curses to the landing our Jordanian pilot had just announced. We would be setting down at Erbil International Airport within moments. Had I not been lost in thought, I would have known how near we were to our destination by simply looking out the window. The Zagros Mountains swept the landscape on the horizon, mountains so ruggedly beautiful that they seemed part of a stage divinely prepared for events of great tragedy and import. It was like no other scenery in the world. No one on that plane who had been there before could be in doubt. Kurdistan lay below.

Our plane descended smoothly. As it did, I realized I was not fully prepared for what lay ahead. I should explain that I had visited Erbil many times before. In fact, I had traveled through much of Kurdistan, but I had not returned since news of the astonishing transformation of the Kurdish homeland began to fill news reports the world over—since "To the Kurdish Miracle" had become a toast commonly heard in Washington and London. I realized in the moments before touchdown I still had the Kurds frozen in my mind as they had been decades before. I had not allowed the new to overwrite the old. I had set myself up for a life-changing surprise.

I shook these reflections from my mind as I descended the steps from the plane. I confess my next thought was that the pilot had missed Erbil and landed in hell. It was nearly 110 degrees and hotter still on the sizzling tarmac.

The heat quickly left my mind as I was driven through the city streets. I had never imagined Erbil could become such a place. The most I had been able to envision when I heard of Kurdistan's economic revolution were stores with well-stocked shelves, roads without murderous potholes, and a smattering of new construction.

Instead, I left a newly built world-class airport and drove by five-star hotels and office towers taller than anything in my hometowns of Nashville and Washington, DC. The newest cars from a dozen nations were common sights. Luxurious restaurants, richly provisioned grocery stores, lovely city parks, gorgeous monuments, and quiet, elegant neighborhoods were everywhere.

I confess that I wept, though it was not just for what I could see. I had known an earlier time. Where lovers strolled, families had once grieved their dead in the rubble of their own homes. Giant machines marked out the footprints of schools and hospitals where children once begged for food.

Such speed of progress and spread of liberty would have been impressive in any part of any nation on the earth. I visited a private school with thousands of students in which classes were conducted only in English, standards were high, and some graduates went on to the finest universities in Europe. I had the good fortune to be in an official's office when news arrived that the public schools of Kurdistan would no longer favor Islam. Under a new ruling, all religions would be taught equally. Extensive knowledge of Islam would no longer be required for graduation. My Muslim host and his aides celebrated this decision like American Pentecostals, hands raised to heaven and tears streaming. Later, I sat with the Senior Mullah of Kurdistan while he assured me he was a Kurd first, a Muslim second. I joked that we might both be killed for his views as we sat together in his office. He said, quietly, "Then let it come if it is the will of Allah. But it will not come. This is Kurdistan."

Strolling the streets, I found the people grateful, eager, and filled with hope. I spoke with merchants who excitedly described plans for Erbil to become an international shopping and entertainment destination like Dubai. Cheap fuel would bring planes from every nation, they assured. Businessmen spoke breathlessly of the 2006 law removing any distinction between foreign and domestic investment in Kurdistan, a huge welcome mat to investment capital worldwide. They also made sure I knew that the Erbil Stock Exchange had begun tapping NASDAQ's OMX X-stream technology. I was impressed. This was an incisive move, a major step toward assuring that Kurdistan would remain a market economy. No more of the Baathist Nazi-style socialism that had raped the nation for decades.

These milestones were likely the reason men in teashops lectured me about the difference between the south of Iraq and Kurdistan. "Tell them when you go home," they demanded. They worried that killings and civil unrest in Baghdad would obscure hard-won victories in places like Erbil, Duhok and Sulimaniya. "America must know," they insisted. "You tell them."

Kurds I had met on the streets for five minutes were eager to show me their version of Kurdistan. A shopkeeper wanted to close down his business for the day to take me to a monument Kurds had built to the American dead. A businessman wanted me to understand that Kurdish warriors—called *Peshmerga* or "those who face death"—were not the bumblers the Iraqi trainees in the south were proving to be. These warriors took target practice while standing on one leg to hone their combat skills and could survive in the mountains for months at a time if required. They were true soldiers. My businessman friend knew a high-ranking commander. They would allow me to observe. A family that ran a baklava shop—where I embarrassed myself with purchases nearly every day—told me I had not seen Kurdistan until I had seen their village nestled by a lake in the mountains. They would take me. I would be welcome.

Then came the conversation that led to this book. A writer who had lived in Los Angeles and spoke English nearly as well as I did stepped into one of my street conversations to interpret for me. As we finished and were walking away, he rounded out another man's point by explaining that Iraq is the size of California. Culturally, he explained, the north of Iraq, where the Kurds live, is as remote from Baghdad as southern California is from the farm and ranch region of northern California. This condensed days of conversation into a single image and I was grateful.

It was what the young writer said next, as he shook my hand at the entrance to my hotel, that has never left me. He could tell I was swimming in a million facts and a thousand bits of conversation. He wanted to cut through it all. "What you must know" he said kindly, but with piercing seriousness, "is that Kurdistan is what America wanted Iraq to be. Kurdistan is America's reward."

I sat up late that last night in Kurdistan to ponder this. I should say here that though I have written about politics and military affairs in the United States, I have no special pipeline of information. My vantage point is very much from the edge. I was embedded for a season with U.S. troops in Iraq because I had written *The Faith of George W. Bush* and was known to the officials at the Pentagon whose permission I needed to enter that theater of operations. I also speak from time to time at West Point, the Naval Academy, and the Pentagon. Beyond that, I live in Washington, DC, and have some friends who are policy makers and some who command troops. I've also had the sad honor of attending the funerals of our war dead at Arlington National Cemetery.

None of this makes me an expert or gives me any authority with which to speak of military affairs. None of it makes me privy to the counsel offered to a commander-in-chief by his inner circle of advisors or to a commanding general by his staff. Yet with this openly acknowledged, when my young Kurdish writer friend spoke, I had just enough perspective from my perch on the edge of officialdom to know that he was right. *Kurdistan is what America wanted from the war. Kurdistan is America's reward.*

During the recent war in Iraq, when the American president or a commander at Camp Victory or a senator on a Sunday morning talk show spoke of their hopes for the future of Iraq, it was what Kurdistan has become and is becoming that they were envisioning. It was what the Kurds are building that U.S. leaders were hoping for, whether they knew it or not. This is also what many of our troops were envisioning. I know because I asked them and I often asked them moments before they roared off in their Humvees down IED-strewn roads to put their lives at risk. What Kurdistan is today is what many of our troops embraced as the vision for "Iraqi freedom" worth their sacrifice—even though most had never even heard of Kurdistan at the time.

It is because Kurdistan symbolizes this galvanizing vision of our hopes for the Middle East—and because her phoenixlike rise from the ashes of history has power to inspire our own ascents—that hers is tale that ought to be told. It is a story I want my children and grandchildren to know. It is a saga I want the dismissed and despised tribes of the world to hear and to be inspired by. It is also a majestic morality tale I hope even kings and congresses will ponder. These are the only reasons I have dared to write this little book.

I should be quick to say that there will be, in time, far more skillful accounts of the Kurdish journey than this one. Eminent scholars and brilliant analysts will eventually turn to the history and recent rise of the Kurds and illuminate its meaning for generations to come, perhaps even for generations of the Kurds themselves. I hope for that day. I pray for it.

Yet, there is value in even an informal retelling of this story now—while the miracle is still transpiring, the blood is still moist in the soil and the tears still come.

I played no major role in the rise of the Kurds. I did have the privilege of knowing some of the giants of that ascent—statesman and missionaries, courageous men and heroic women, magnificent priests and mullahs. I was not among them. My only qualifications are that I was near enough to notice and I was ignorant enough be deeply impressed with all I heard and saw. And I had a pen.

Still, I saw what most could not and I cannot imagine allowing any of it to die a death of silence. I cannot fail to speak, for example, of a man like Mansour Hussein, who died of a bullet to the head simply for daring to man a fledgling Christian bookstore. I do not want to keep silent about the good the Roman Catholic Church did in one episode involving the Kurds. When Protestant/Catholic tensions arose in Kurdistan and a few American evangelicals traveled to Rome to appeal to the Vatican for help, that help came. Changes were made. The church's embrace of what Pope John Paul II called his "departed brethren"—Protestants—was warm and lasting. In an age of very public scandals within the Catholic church, this, too, ought to be remembered.

Nor would I want the sweet stories of the children I knew to be lost. One small boy was so traumatized by the violence around him that his little eight-year-old personality nearly split in two. I happened to be visiting not long after. Having nothing else to offer, I decided to become the rowdy older brother it seemed the child needed. For days on end I kicked soccer balls, petted chickens, chased dogs, and played hide-and-seek until the boy fell exhausted into my arms. For one entire day, I watched him unpack my suitcase, get in the suitcase, then get out of the suitcase and repack it again. This he did over and over. I wondered if he was trying to fit his world together again. Perhaps he subconsciously wanted me to take him to my home safely on the other side of the world. My young friend recovered himself over time, but it was heartbreaking to see him so shattered and heartbreaking also to know that there were many terrified children just like him throughout Kurdistan.

These and a thousand stories like them are important—not because they happened within my reach but because they happened among the Kurds, a people soon to become, perhaps, the world's newest nation. Their story, and every story within that story, is part of a great beginning, and it has power to inspire still other beginnings yet to come.

It is a tale that belongs to all people, but I confess I am particularly eager for my own countrymen to know the Kurdish story. The United States has emerged from the recent war in Iraq largely convinced, if opinion polls are any guide, that its sons and daughters died in vain in that land, as did the young of other nations. It is not true. Whatever the virtues of the policies that sent young warriors into battle and whatever else comes of their sacrifices, the liberation of Kurdistan and the promise of her future is at least a partial answer to the dear losses endured by so many.

On the last day of that visit to Kurdistan, I was again walking the streets, eager to remember all that I had seen. Kurdish hospitality stalked me. I tasted baklava offered by generous merchants, asked the Arabic names of the most unusual fresh vegetables and picked a humorous argument with the owner of a sporting goods shop about whether a white ball with black spots had anything to do with the true game of football. "Better than NFL," he said with delight.

Then I came to the sight that amazed me. Rounding a corner, I came upon a—well, a jam store. It was, I tell you, a store that mainly sold jam and from all over the world. I entered the little shop. The merchant approached. I gestured widely with my hands and said with a look of surprise, "So much jam!" I hoped he understood. He did. "Yes. Yes. Much jam. Much jam." I looked around for a moment. How could I explain to him what jam could symbolize? Again, I gestured.

"In all Kurdistan?" I asked. "Duhok? Mosul?" A voice from the back of the shop helped the merchant understand what I had asked. "Yes. Yes." he said. Then, stepping toward me to signal he was about to say something important. "We hev jem," he said, "be cuz thera eez jem." *We have jam, because there is jam. There is jam in the world, so now we have jam in Kurdistan. All that is in the world can now be ours.*

I can just see that merchant telling his friends over tea about the odd American who brushed away tears while he bought more jam than anyone could possibly need. I don't care. God bless him anyway. We have jam.

CHAPTER 2

THE TIMES OF THE KURDISH PEOPLE

"The measure of an education is that you acquire some idea of the extent of your ignorance. And it seems at least thinkable that today's history students don't quite know what subject they are not being taught."

—Christopher Hitchens[1]

I have spoken a great deal about the Kurds in my life. On more than one occasion, I have had to distinguish for an American audience between *Kurds*, the people who populate Kurdistan, and *curds*, the breakfast food that has a starring role in the famous nursery rhyme—"Little Miss Muffet, sat on her tuffet, eating her curds and whey." I have had less disturbing moments in my life.

We Americans love what we know of the history of the world but we still have much to learn. This can leave us ill-equipped to contend well on the modern global stage and it can keep us from appreciating both the power and the possibilities in a story like that of the Kurds. This embodies my great fear for my countrymen—not just that we will have to repeat the history we do not know, as George Santayana predicted, but that in lacking much knowledge of the past we will find little of value in the history we do know.

I understand what it is to hate learning about the past. My complaint has long been that history as it is usually taught is merely "dates and dead people," or, as Shakespeare wrote in *Macbeth*, a "tale, told by an idiot, full of sound and fury, signifying nothing."

We should admit, though, that our national spite for history has much to do with the classroom version and little to do with the actual events and adventures that have preceded us. There is every indication—from the popularity of historical movies to attendance figures at historical theme parks—that Americans can grow to love history once given a taste of the genuine article.

Only in this hope would I dare to include a timeline like this one at the beginning of a book. Such things are usually hidden neatly away at the back of books, as though to assure they will never be seen. My hope here, though, is that this flyover of the Kurdish journey will provide the not-too-dull introduction to a tale that is filled with epic battles and religious passion, with vile betrayals and defining loyalties, and with a fierce people's undying dream of freedom.

6300 BC

The rugged, magnificent land of Kurdistan was probably first home to the Hurrian people. Our knowledge of these Hurrians is sketchy, but they were likely among the first human beings to cultivate crops and domesticate animals—mainly dogs for hunting. We know also that they buried their dead in caves, adorned graves with flowers, and, to the lasting gratitude of their descendants, learned to brew beer.

3000 BC

The first written mention of the Kurds occurred in a Sumerian document that described "the land of Kardo." These were a people known for tending flocks in the isolation of their mountains and for their astonishing warrior skills. They seemed content to let the wider world pass them by. It was a luxury that would not last. In time, the Akkadians, the Assyrians, the Babylonians, the Parthians, the

Persians, the Romans, and the Armenians would claim all or part of the Kurds and their land.

2000 BC

It was at this time that the history we witness in the pages of the Bible began overlaying the land of Kurdistan. The patriarch Abraham passed through this region in his trek from Ur of the Chaldees to the "Promised Land." Later, the Assyrian Empire ruled this same region from Nineveh—now Mosul, a city familiar to the West from news reports of Iraq's recent wars—and it was to this ancient city that the eighth-century BC prophet Jonah roared his warnings.

612 BC

An army of Medes and Persians overthrew the Assyrian Empire. After the fall of the Assyrian capitol, Nineveh, the powerful Mede kingdom extended its territory from the highlands of what is now Iran to the central plateau of what is now Turkey. With its capital at Ecbatana in the foothills of the Zagros Mountains and near the modern Iranian city of Hamadan, the Mede Kingdom became—along with Babylonia, Lydia, and Egypt—one of the four greatest powers of the ancient Near East.

550 BC

The Medes were conquered by Cyrus the Great, founder of the Persian Achaemenid Empire. As part of this empire, these Medes—referred to also as the "Carduchians" or "Gordions" or "Kurds"—displayed their warrior genius in the many legendary wars of Persia. The great chronicler of the Greek wars with Persia, Herodotus, described the courage, ferocity, and cunning of the Mede troops.

During these tumultuous centuries, the Northern Kingdom of ancient Israel was conquered by Assyria nearly two hundred years before all ancient Israel was conquered by Babylon. The Hebrews then lived in a Babylonian exile for seventy years before many of them—but certainly not all—returned to their land by the good graces of Persia. Not too many generations would pass before they were ruled in turn by the Greeks and then the Romans.

522 BC

Darius the Great, the son of an Imperial Satrap from the Kurdish lands, overthrew the Achaemenid emperor and inaugurated the new Empire of the Medes and the Persians. He was among the greatest rulers of the ancient world. He extended his dominion from the Indus Valley in the east to Macedonia and Libya in the west, from the Caspian Sea in the north to the Arabian Peninsula in the south. The greatness of Darius was chronicled in the Greek histories of Herodotus as well as the Biblical books of Ezra, Nehemiah, Daniel, Haggai, and Zechariah.

64 AD

Christianity was born after the death of Jesus Christ and entered Kurdish realms largely through the ministries of the apostles Thomas and Thaddeus, two of the disciples of Christ. Thomas was one of the original twelve apostles of Jesus and Thaddeus was one of the first seventy disciples described in the Gospel of Luke. Their work began proving successful just twenty years after the crucifixion of Jesus. The Christian communities these apostles founded in what is now Iraq and Iran have continued with varying degrees of vitality and influence to this day.

325

Representatives from throughout the Kurdish region joined hundreds of other churchmen, theologians, and diplomats at the famed Council of Nicaea. During this first "Ecumenical Council" of the Christian Church, the Nicene Creed was formulated—a statement of faith that has been used by many Christians ever since.

431

At the Church's third Ecumenical Council at Ephesus, the gathered pastors and theologians condemned the teachings of Nestorius, a controversial preacher and bishop who was particularly popular in Kurdish lands. Eventually, this led to these "Nestorian Churches" being isolated from the Eastern Orthodox and Roman Catholic Churches of the West.

622

This date marks the official beginning of Islam under the prophet Muhammad. Slightly more than a decade later, Muhammad died knowing that his new monotheistic religion ruled the Arabian Peninsula. A century later, Islam ruled so much of the known world that it pressed hard upon the gates of an increasingly divided Europe.

637

Muslim armies under the Caliph Umar began an invasion of the Persian heartland. After a series of fierce battles, the last Sassanid emperor, Yazdegerd III, was overthrown. This inevitably led to the slow decline of the then-dominant Zoroastrian religion in Persia. Over time, the majority of the people converted to Islam, though a vigorous Christian community continued.

830

Kurdish dynasties began appearing about this time. Seljuk Sultan Sandjar "Turk" annexed seventeen Kurdish principalities by 1150 and established the "Kurdistan Province." A Kurdish "Ayyubid" dynasty began arising within Islam, known for its resistance to Christian crusaders and its benevolent policies toward Jews.

1168

Kurdish warrior, Saladin, became the Sultan of Egypt and Syria. He skillfully united the Islamic world, defeated the Crusaders, reclaimed Jerusalem, and signed peace treaties with the European powers. He ruled until his death in 1193 and is revered as the greatest of Kurds to this day. His encounters with Richard the Lionheart of England during the Third Crusade were legendary and became the theme of troubadours' songs and chivalric adventure stories (or *chansons de geste*) during the Medieval period.

1453

Constantinople, a largely Christian city ruled by the Byzantine Empire, fell to the Muslim Ottoman armies of Muhammad II. The Ottoman Empire then turned its attention eastward and not long afterward began invading Kurdish lands. This conquest would be slow and halting as the Kurds took to a nomadic existence high in the Zagros Mountains.

1839

Scottish missionaries, inspired by the vision of their mentor, Thomas Chalmers, ventured into the Kurdish region to establish schools and churches. Several of these Presbyterian communities survive to this day in cities like Kirkuk, Sulimaniya, and Erbil.

1880

Infuriated by the brutal conquest of the last autonomous Kurdish tribal lands, the widely scattered Kurds revolted against the Ottoman Provincial Government. Under the leadership of Sheikh Said, a new Kurdish national identity began to take shape.

1920

After the defeat of the Ottoman Empire in World War I, the victorious European powers placed

Kurdistan under a British mandate and agreed to the Treaty of Sevres at a peace conference in Paris. The spirit of this treaty drew from U.S. President Woodrow Wilson's "Fourteen Points"—his guiding principles for the post-war world—which urged that "nationalities which are now under Turkish rule should be assured an undoubted security of life and an absolutely unmolested opportunity of autonomous development." The birth of a Kurdish nation seemed possible.

1923

In their eager negotiations for the creation of a Turkish Republic, the European powers bartered away all guarantees of Kurdish independence. The Treaty of Lausanne, which superseded the stillborn Treaty of Sevres, failed to even mention the Kurds. Understandably, the Kurds considered this a betrayal and revolted. Kemal Ataturk's new Turkish Republic responded with a brutal crusade of suppression that lasted for decades and left thousands of decimated Kurdish villages in its wake. Kurdish identity itself became a target. In time, Kurdish language, Kurdish dress, Kurdish literature, and even use of the word *Kurd* were outlawed under Turkish law.

Kurdish revolts continued, the most promising occurring under Sheikh Mahmoud Barzani, who declared himself "King of the Kingdom of Kurdistan." This revolt was suppressed largely at British insistence. Sheikh Barzani was forced into exile.

1931

A royal Kurdish family from Northern Kurdistan, the Bedirxans, was forced into exile in Syria. While there, they established the Kurdish National League, sponsored Kurdish publications and fostered the creation of a Kurdish Latin-character alphabet. These were each major steps forward in the preservation of Kurdish culture and identity.

1946

During World War II, the Allied Powers invaded Iran, leaving the Soviet Union largely in control of the northern part of the country. Seizing the moment, Kurdish leaders declared an independent "Republic of Mahabad" and appealed to the Soviets for support.

Suspicious of Soviet intentions, the United States opposed this move, preferring an independent, unified Iran to an Iran under Soviet control. Hopes for Kurdish independence were crushed. The Shah of Iran then ordered the arrest and execution of Kurdish leaders. One of these leaders was Mustafa Barzani, the first president of the Kurdistan Democratic Party (KDP), founded to support the Mahabad Republic. To escape the Shah's oppressive hand, Barzani fled into exile in the Soviet Union.

1958

The monarchy that had ruled Iraq with British support since World War I fell to a military coup. General Abdel Karim Qassem became the new president. A provisional constitution proclaimed, "Arabs and Kurds are considered partners in this homeland." In this spirit, the new president invited Mustafa Barzani to return from his Soviet exile.

Sadly, the Iraqi government quickly proved unstable and treacherous. The Kurds were again oppressed, prompting Mustafa Barzani to lead a series of revolts.

1961

Suspicious of Barzani's influence and hoping to prevent a Kurdish uprising, Qassem ordered air assaults on Kurdish towns. Barzani responded by leading the Iraqi Kurds in open revolt against the government.

1968

After a series of coups, ousters, and accidental deaths, General Ahmed Hassan al-Bakr became the president of Iraq. Foolishly, he appointed an ambitious minor official as chief of his bodyguards. This man's name was Saddam Hussein. Soon after, Saddam demanded officer's rank in the Iraqi army and, inexplicably, was made a four-star general despite his complete lack of military training.

1970

An agreement between the Iraqi government and Kurdish leaders recognized Kurdish as the second official language of Iraq after Arabic. The constitution was also amended to read, "the Iraqi people is made up of two nationalities, the Arab nationality and the Kurdish nationality."

1971

Once again, in the history of the Kurds, the Iraqi government shifted its attitude toward the Kurds and began denying their rights as citizens. Mustafa Barzani appealed to the United States for aid.

1974

In the first of many reversals damaging to the Kurds, the United States first supported KDP attempts to take control of the oil-rich Kirkuk province of Kurdistan/northern Iraq and then suddenly ended that support. Abandoned by the Western nations, Kurdish revolts were violently suppressed by the Iraqi Baath Regime.

1975

Jalal Talabani, a former member of the KDP, established a second Kurdish political party, the Patriotic Union of Kurdistan (PUK).

The Algiers Accord between Iran and Iraq ended Iranian support for the Kurdish uprising. Abandoned, the Kurdish resistance collapsed.

Increasingly in ill health, Mustafa Barzani fled first to Iran and then to the United States for medical care.

1979

Saddam Hussein forced President Al-Bakr out of power and declared himself president and prime minister of Iraq.

An Islamic revolution began in Iran. Kurdish independence movements in that country were quickly suppressed by the new regime.

Indicative of Turkish oppression of the Kurds, the mayor of Diyarbakir, a large city in eastern Turkey, received a ten-year prison sentence for writing Kurdish poetry and advocating Kurdish rights.

Mustafa Barzani died of cancer. His son, Massoud Barzani, assumed control of the KDP.

1980

The disastrous, decade-long, Iran-Iraq war began. It proved to be one of the bloodiest, costliest wars in history. During the conflict, the KDP provided aid to Iran along the northern Iraqi border while the PUK negotiated with Baghdad.

1983

The Iraqi Baath regime under Saddam Hussein attacked Kurdish villages with chemical weapons. Eight thousand Kurds were killed.

1986

The PUK and KDP unified and formed the "Kurdish Front" against Baghdad.

1988

Saddam launched his murderous *"Al-Anfal"* campaign against Iraqi Kurds. More than 182,000 Kurds were killed during this hellish time. Chemical weapons were used against several Kurdish cities, including Halabjah in which nearly 5000 Kurds were killed in a matter of hours and another 7000 died in the weeks afterward.

1990

Saddam Hussein ordered Iraqi troops into Kuwait. A disputed territory since the days of the post-World War I British Mandate, Kuwait was a strategic strip of land along the Persian Gulf long claimed by Saddam for Iraq. The United Nations, the United States, and most of the rest of the world disagreed. The result was the 100-hour "Persian Gulf War" which liberated Kuwait and crippled Saddam's vast Iraqi army.

1991

As the Persian Gulf War neared an end, the Kurds heeded U.S. President George H. W. Bush's call for an Iraqi uprising against Saddam Hussein. Once again, the Kurds were nearly abandoned by the Western nations and met with murderous reprisals from Iraqi forces. The Kurds took to their mountains.

More than a million and a half Kurds fled to either Turkey or Iran. En route, they starved and died of disease and exposure. In time, the United States and the United Kingdom established a no-fly zone over most of Iraqi Kurdistan to protect the Kurds from air assault. Massoud Barzani of the KDP and Jalal Talabani of the PUK quickly took control of the provinces within the no-fly zone. A *de facto* Kurdish state began to exist in northern Iraq.

1992

Turkey moved thirty thousand troops into Iraqi Kurdistan in pursuit of the guerrilla forces of the Kurdistan Workers' Party (PKK) and its leader, Abdullah Öcalan.

1994

A civil war for territorial control erupted between the KDP and the PUK. It continued for four years, deeply damaging the Kurdish cause in the eyes of the international community.

1995

The United Nations launched its "Oil-for-Food" program in which Iraq was permitted to sell its oil on world markets in exchange for food, medicine, and other humanitarian needs that were in short supply due to economic sanctions.

2001

Abdullah Öcalan, leader of the PKK, was captured in Nairobi, Kenya, and returned to Turkey for trial.

2003

In the aftermath of the September 11, 2001, al Qaeda attacks on the United States, a coalition of countries led by the U.S. initiated Operation Iraqi Freedom to overthrow Saddam Hussein. Coalition forces occupied Iraq within a month, though hostilities continued for years. On April 9, a statue of Saddam Hussein was famously torn down in Baghdad's Fardus Square. On December 13, Saddam was found hiding in a hole near his hometown of Tikrit.

2005

A new Iraqi constitution was approved by 79 percent of voters and hailed as the first democratic national charter in Arab history. Jalal Talabani, leader of the PUK, became the first democratically elected and Kurdish president of Iraq. Massoud Barzani, leader of the KDP, became the president of the autonomous Kurdistan Regional Government.

Massoud Barzani inaugurated the first session of Kurdistan's reunified parliament.

With the advent of the no-fly zone, the Kurds had steadily prospered and wisely invested in regional development. Their economic progress was years ahead of the rest of Iraq. The new Iraqi constitution allowed for even more rapid growth. Soon, the western press began touting the "Kurdish Miracle." In Erbil alone, a massive and ultra-modern airport, shopping malls, Western-style grocery stores, five-star hotels, and gleaming office buildings signaled a new day for Kurdistan. Regional government policies designed to attract foreign investment served to transform what was once a town huddled around an ancient citadel into a teeming twenty-first century city.

2006

An "Investment Law," approved by the Kurdistan National Assembly and ratified by President Massoud Barzani, ingeniously laid the foundation for much of modern Kurdistan's prosperity. The law granted foreign investors equal status to indigenous investors, huge tax breaks, and full rights of ownership and profit. When the law was announced, billions of investment dollars poured into Kurdistan, creating jobs, elevating the standard of living, and dramatically accelerating the Kurdish economic miracle.

2013

Among the most significant indicators of Kurdistan's economic development and political stability was the inclusion of the region on "must-see" travel lists. *The New York Times, National Geographic Traveler,* and *Condé Nast* each touted Kurdistan as among the most enjoyable and important places for tourists to visit in the second decade of the new millennium.

During the Syrian Civil War, tens of thousands of Syrian refugees—many of them Syrian Kurds—poured into Kurdistan. The Kurdish Regional Government—mentioning often in official statements that the Kurds of Kurdistan knew well what refugees were forced to endure—welcomed these Syrian refugees and spent vast sums on their care. The "people without a friend," as the Kurds were often called, had become stable and prosperous enough to provide safe haven to the dispossessed. The world took note of Kurdistan's rising strength and its generous spirit.

Fathers of Modern Kurdistan

MULLAH MUSTAFA BARZANI

On the wall of nearly every government office in Kurdistan, as well as on the wall of most homes, restaurants, and shops, is a photograph of Mullah Mustafa Barzani. He is the closest figure the Kurds have to a George Washington.

The standard version of this photo shows "Mullah Mustafa," as the Kurds affectionately call him, dressed in khaki and gun belt, his dagger always visible, his fierce visage turned to the horizon as though contemplating a Kurdistan of the imagination and the heart. This photo could be called "The Spirit of Kurdistan," for Mullah Mustafa is certainly the spirit who has inspired much of the Kurdish struggle in the last century.

He was born in the village of Barzan on March 14, 1903, to a family of ferocious Kurdish patriots. His father, his grandfather, and a brother were all executed for insurrection by Ottoman authorities. At the age of five, Mustafa Barzani was jailed with his mother. He liked to quip throughout his life that he was suckled in a Turkish jail.

In his twenties he joined his brother, Sheikh Ahmed Barzani, in an ultimately failed uprising against Baghdad's oppressive rule. He was held in internal exile in Sulimaniya until well into World War II and then helped found the Mahabad Republic in Iran, the first declared Kurdish state in history. It would not live long. In 1946, the president of the fledgling republic was hanged and Mustafa Barzani was forced into exile in Azerbaijan, then a part of the Soviet Union. His fifty-two day journey at the lead of two hundred men—on foot through mountains and freezing weather, occasionally fighting both the Turkish and Iranian armies—is a story Kurdish mothers tell their young. His eleven-year Soviet exile did not endear him in the United States, where government officials dubbed him "the Red Mullah."

A coup in Iraq in 1958 took Barzani back to Iraq where he survived revolutions, fought unceasingly for Kurdish rights, pled for Western support, endured repeated betrayals from the West, and traveled widely to declare the Kurdish cause. He died in Washington, DC, in 1979, his coalition fraying, an Islamic revolution rising in Iran, and his people endangered by the rise of Saddam Hussein. Still, his passion for his people and his many sacrifices rallied even those who disagreed with him to serve the Kurdish people. He is, as visitors are told often in Kurdistan today, "The Father of the Kurd."

CHAPTER 3

AKY, AKY HARTZ

"Lacking an alternative homeland of any kind,
Kurds can emigrate, but they can't escape."
—Christopher Hitchens[1]

Imet my first Kurd in Nashville, Tennessee. There is a story about how Kurds first arrived in Nashville. It's a good one.

The U.S. military was relocating Kurds after the Persian Gulf War to protect them from Saddam Hussein's genocidal campaign against them. As the story goes, a grizzled transportation sergeant asked a Kurdish elder where he wanted to take his family. Where would he like for them to start their new life outside of Kurdistan?

As the story goes, the old man did not hesitate. Nashville, Tennessee. The cigar-chomping sergeant looked perplexed and asked why. The aged Kurd explained through an interpreter that just the day before he had seen his grandchildren dancing joyously to a song playing on an American soldier's radio. The moment brought tears to the man's eyes. He had not seen his grandchildren so carefree in months. That evening he asked them what music they were listening to while they danced with such abandon. The excited children explained that the song was a very popular one in America. It was called "Aky, Aky Hartz." The singer was "Billee Raz Ceeraz." It was music from a city in America called "Nasveel." The music was called "Cantree" music. Very famous American music. We love it, grandpa.

Hoping to choose a future for his people where the children would be happy—the young ones had already endured all the terrors of a lifetime—the man lifted his head regally and declared, "Take us to where that music lives!" And with a smile and a disbelieving shake of the head, the sergeant put the first Kurds on a series of flights to Music City USA—Nashville, Tennessee.

It is a wonderful story and it is sometimes still told in Nashville. How wonderful to believe that the thousands of Kurds who now live in Music City USA came because they were drawn by the music—even the outlier hit "Achy Breaky Heart" by Billy Ray Cyrus, one of the biggest-selling songs in country music history.

How nice it would be—if, in fact, it were true. It likely isn't. How could it be? Who would have recounted it to eager ears in the United States? That sergeant would have told the story at a bar somewhere and then forgotten all about it. Aging as he was, the chief likely never left Kurdistan and so would not have been the one to carry the tale abroad.

The truth is that the Kurds first began showing up in Nashville in 1976. They had taken part in a failed attempt to overthrow the government of Iraq and were fleeing the inevitable payback. They came in intermittent waves afterward, the largest of which occurred during the early 1990s when thousands fled Iraq to escape Saddam Hussein's vicious *Anfal.* Middle Tennessee's climate, prosperity and hospitality, as well as the urging of Kurds who already called the Athens of the South their home, made Nashville an inviting refuge. Now she claims over ten thousand Kurds, more than any other U.S. city, and her good-hearted people have resigned themselves to yet another nickname: Little Kurdistan.

It is a tribute to the people of Tennessee, their churches in particular, that the Kurds were welcomed with such warmth. Fresh from war-ravaged villages, most of these Kurds had nothing when they first landed blinking and overwhelmed at the Nashville International Airport. Few spoke English, few were familiar with the Western world, few were well-educated, and most could not have located Nashville on a map. They were exhausted, confused, and in need of nearly every essential of life.

Volunteers from the Volunteer State got busy and began helping the new arrivals to learn English, get driver's licenses, and find jobs. One organization, understanding something of Kurdish culture, built teahouses and shipped in tea, pistachio nuts, and backgammon boards by the crateful. These became hubs of transplanted Kurdish life. Another charity start-up raised money for college scholarships. Students at one of Nashville's seventeen colleges and universities launched a program to sell Kurdish crafts and clothes. There seemed to be no limits to the creative variety of Tennessee's generosity.

I was there in the 1990s as Kurds began pouring into Nashville. At first, I was no more than an interested onlooker. Like many others, I gave a bit of my time and money to ease the transition of these traumatized refugees. I was there, but that was all. I did not start or lead the charities that served the Kurds in Nashville. I did not start or lead the agencies that worked among the Kurds in Iraq. At most, I can say that I was there. I knew a bit of history. I had a writer's fascination with the imprint life leaves upon the soul. I was ignorant of all things Kurdish—which means that I was impressionable. That was all.

I had, though, traveled widely by then and seen something of hardship and brutality in the world. Never had I seen grief, weariness, and longing so dramatically etched into human faces as I did when I first met Kurds in Nashville. Never had I seen a people so lost, so proud, and so grateful for a friend. Once I spent time among them and once I discovered that the unofficial Kurdish motto is simply, "The Kurds have no friends," I wanted to help break the curse. Their great need and magnificent spirit drew this from me. I soon met others who were won to the Kurds in much the same way.

I was desperate to understand them. Language, the vast chasm between our cultures, and their overwhelming grief fought against it. I eventually concluded that my best chance of understanding the Kurds was to just find one I could befriend. I decided that a male young enough to have fought in the war but old enough to remember well would serve best, particularly if he was angry and eager to tell his story. Nearly all Kurds were. After gallons of tea, pounds of pistachio nuts, and constant humiliation at the backgammon board, I found a man I could understand with only occasional help from an interpreter. His name was Asan. He was my gateway and my first guide to that world he called simply, "the Kurd." Using what I learned from this fiery man, from my reading, and from what experienced aid workers taught me, I began piecing together the journey of a people that seemed to touch all the torment and dignity humanity has to offer.

It was easy to listen to Asan. He was fiercely handsome, with dark features and eyes made brilliant by flashes of his anger and his hurt. Of average height and weight, he was well-muscled in that compact, agile way of warriors. He kept his black hair short and well-trimmed and his moustache the same way.

In this, he was like most every other Kurdish male on earth. By custom, Kurdish men are nearly always impeccably groomed. So devoted are they to this cause that they routinely tend to one another's grooming. Even in wartime and even in the most rustic outpost, somewhere there are a handful of men gathered around a chair and talking about the latest news while one of their number receives a precise and time-honored barber treatment from a fellow warrior. The result is impressive. A friend traveling with me in Kurdistan once said, "My God, here we are in a war zone and there's not a bad haircut in sight." A more cynical acquaintance thundered, "It's like I've died and gone to hell at a New York waiter's convention."

Asan captured my attention with a range of facial expressions I later learned were shared by most Kurdish men. When I first approached him to introduce myself, he glared at me with such ferocity that it actually crossed my mind that he might want to kill me. We were standing in front of a Nashville Smoothie King at the time, not on some battlefield in Iraq. Yet once I became his friend, his face exploded into such a look of joy and goodwill when he saw me that I felt grateful to be in his favor. It was the same when a Kurd approached. Asan was scowling and tense until the stranger gave the traditional Kurdish salute—a right hand held just above the head in a sort of stiff wave—and then came all the charm and warmth a man's face can reveal.

He was thirty years old when I met him and he began describing his life to me. He came into the world, then, a few years after Iraq overthrew the monarchy that had ruled it since just after World War I. His earliest memories were of his parents and other elders speaking in urgent terms about the revolutions, assassinations, and political intrigue that plagued their people. Long before he should have been required to, he absorbed one of the great defining realities of his life: there were many in the world who despised him simply for being a Kurd. He felt early the rage of men like his father over the stinging reality that they were part of the largest people group on earth without a homeland of their own. This anger blended with Asan's innate ferocity and his mystical, poetic nature to make him one of the most complicated, endearing men I've ever known. But then this is simply a wordy way of saying Asan was a Kurd—most all of whom are fierce, angry, mystical, poetic and, without doubt, complicated.

By the time he entered his twenties, he understood the evils long visited upon his people. He knew, for example, of the gassings. He understood that his nation's president had ordered them. He knew fellow tribesmen who had survived them. He had also learned the extent of them—that tens of thousands had already died and in indescribable agony. There is no comprehending from our great geographic and emotional distance what this must have done to him.

What he had been told of these horrors lived jaggedly in his mind. On one rainy Nashville afternoon, Asan described to me what had befallen a Kurdish village near his hometown. It had been a quiet weekday. Young boys urged goats through the streets. Women scolded children and hung laundry out to dry. As he spoke, Asan seemed to hear a child's cry and the sound of the village tractor and the snarling of scraggly, unwelcome dogs. This was life as he knew it in Kurdistan and so what came next in his story was all the more torturous to him. I could see him straining for the right words. He wanted me to feel as well as to hear.

What he could hear and likely would all his days was the sound of artillery. He knew it would not have raised much alarm in the village that day. It was not unexpected and was usually harmless. Yet this time, there was a difference.

Something was missing. There was no explosion, only the initial roar of the guns. No sound seemed to follow. It was as though the shells continued their upward path without ever falling to earth.

A few villagers knew what this meant, but by the time they began to scream to the others it was too late. Most did not realize anything was wrong until they noticed one of two very strange occurrences.

The first was what started happening to the birds. They were falling to the ground by the hundreds. Those villagers who survived the day said later that it seemed as though the sky was raining birds. They would always be haunted by the dull thump of bird bodies striking the ground. Their nightmares would remind them of the ghostly whistling sound the creatures made trying to breathe and the sight of beaks slowly opening and closing like scissors in unsteady hands.

Asan spoke of these things with a kind of hushed horror. He had not been there on that horrible day, but he had relived it again and again in the retelling. Always, there were tears and convulsions that would not allow him to speak. This made me wonder if he, too, had survived a chemical attack. He shook his head. No, but he had often held terrified children while they screamed their hellish memories through the night. "I know these things," Asan would say. "I know what they did."

The other oddity of that day in the village was the almost soundless falling of canisters. They were the reason no explosions answered the guns. Their impact on the ground was signaled by a dirty white cloud that soon turned a muddy brown. This cloud did not rise upward like the smoke of cooking fires or a burning field, but slithered sideways like a snake undulating his way out of a box. This darkness clung to the ground and seemed to move like an evil spirit over the village.

The sounds of panic soon slashed the air. What the birds had known in midair began to beset dogs, donkeys, and goats. They screeched out their anguish in a hoarse, intermittent version of their usual sound, all while leaping and contorting wildly. It was as though the animals were possessed. Some whipped about so violently they broke their own necks. Others tried to run, wide-eyed and gasping, until they crashed to the ground and heaved in desperation before dying.

The humans who saw these scenes ran for shelter knowing the cloud reached next for them. They smelled it. It had the stench of rotting fruit. It registered its presence in their eyes first, which felt as though nails were being driven into them. At nearly the same time, the piercing pain in the eyes combined with an intense burning in the nose and an agonizing ache in the throat. Soon, lungs stopped taking in air, joints thickened, and death registered wide-eyed on unmoving faces.

Asan never reached this point in his story without sobbing, but they were the sobs of rage. He was already forming the words that would describe what came next and they seemed to choke him in each retelling. A gas attack on a village during daylight hours was horror enough for a lifetime. Yet Asan knew that the gas also came in the night, while villagers slept. This was because their elders had told them that when the gas came and the brownish-white cloud spread itself vilely over the earth, they should run to the high ground. This would place them above the cloud. Every Kurd knew what to do next. Light fires.

Saddam Hussein knew this, too, and it is the reason he routinely bombarded Kurdish villages with gas canisters in the late night hours. Sleepy children and unsteady adults moved more slowly at night. The nighttime run to the high ground might take twice the usual time. More villagers died during a clumsy, moonlit rush for the nearest hill than did during daylight attacks.

Once the still living made it to the hilltops and lit their fires—just as they began thanking God that Saddam had not taken them this time—they heard the drumming of rotors. It was the sound of Saddam's helicopters. Before the villagers knew what was happening, the gunships were upon them, strafing the bands of fire-lit Kurds who stood helplessly exposed on the high ground that was supposed to be their refuge.

By this point in his story, Asan had no more tears. He stoically described how thousands died in misery. His scowl returning, he spoke of fathers breaking the necks of their own children before the gas or the bullets reached them. He told of families machine-gunned to death by one of their own. It was an act of mercy, Asan assured, not of madness.

All of these images and more lived behind the dark, grief-laden eyes of my fierce Kurdish friend. He urgently wanted me to understand. He sometimes doubted that I could. A madman ruled a demonic regime in the Land Between Two Rivers, the ancient name for what is now Iraq. This was the butchery Asan and his people endured. Could anyone in a place like this America even begin to understand? As my friend ended his tale, I started to comprehend why he seemed so threatening when a stranger approached. I also began to glimpse what a friend might mean to him.

Each time Asan told stories like these, I felt anew how foreign he was. It made me think back to the day he arrived at the Nashville airport. I was there with a group who were committed to greeting new Kurdish arrivals whenever possible. It seemed the least a comfortable people could do for a seemingly unwanted people.

Asan strode warily but confidently from the Delta Airlines jetway. He was wearing the traditional clothing of his people. Most striking was the headdress that looked like a long scarf wrapped in low circles upon his head. He wore a shirt much like the collared shirt any businessman might wear. Over this was what appeared to be a jumpsuit or coverall, though it was usually of higher quality and made of dark green or gray material. This jumpsuit was actually two pieces—a long-tailed shirt and a pair of full, loose-fitting pants—bound together at the waist by a colorful sash that also indicated a man's tribe. Kurds had died in the past for daring to wear such a sash where it was forbidden. Now, particularly now, men like Asan wore it proudly.

From first sight, I found Asan's attire noble and manly, but what captured my eye and my imagination was the incongruity of the images that adorned his weary walk from his plane to claim his baggage. He was from an ancient land and had ancient dreams in his heart. He was only in his early thirties and already his government had tried to kill him, he had fought in a vicious guerrilla war, and had endured the sufferings of a people who are among the most despised on earth. Men had died in his arms. Women had screamed for his help but had died before he could reach them. His mother was one of them.

Now, he walked an airport concourse in the United States with the smell of fast food and the sounds of CNN filling the air. From a nearby wall, Dolly Parton and Porter Wagoner smiled down at him, their dramatic hair and sequined clothing signaling a world entirely apart from anything Asan had known. From a second wall of illuminated ads, a woman dressed only in a bikini stared at our newly arrived Kurd. I learned later that he stared back at the photograph because he had never seen that much of an adult woman's body before. As we reached baggage claim, a high school cheerleading squad noisily welcomed home a victorious team. There was much screaming and hugging before the cheerleaders launched into a dance movement that must have looked to Asan like a tribal mating ritual. He said nothing but stared at the commotion with a look of fear and sadness.

I witnessed several such arrivals of refugees, and each time I pondered what was to me a disturbing mystery: how would people from Kurdish villages in northern Iraq make a home in what many locals liked to call "Nashvegas"?

Time and experience did little to solve this mystery for me. I knew that kindhearted Americans would think of a man like Asan as a man rescued. Initially, I thought just like them. He had come to the land of freedom and of abundance. His life would be better than he could have envisioned before and his children's lives would be more astonishing still. He would learn English, master the art of driving American roads, and find work that would earn him more in a day than his cousins in Kurdistan earned in three months. Perhaps the future offered a house of his own, a college degree, and all that came with being grafted into the American dream.

Yet these kindhearted Americans did not understand—I did not understand—how far removed American culture was from Asan's prior experience and how horribly lonely it all would be for him. I did not think of him as less than those of us who welcomed him. I admired him as a freedom fighter. I honored him as a survivor of the killing fields. I wanted him to live long and well and one day take his grandchildren back to Iraq to dance on Saddam Hussein's grave.

Yet I also saw him as a beginner in this all-important matter of being an American. I saw him as a trainee, as a kind of "pre-American." It never crossed my mind that he landed at the Nashville airport attached to anything he would not happily give up to be—one of us.

I certainly did not expect that Asan and his fellow Kurds would arrive in America with anything to teach me. I'm embarrassed by these words now and would not have said them aloud then. Still, this was my thinking: Kurds were lovable rubes whom we now had a chance to bring into the glories of modernity.

What I could never have imagined then, but now know to be true, is that the Kurds landed in Nashville laden with treasures—treasures born of ancient covenants and punishing wars, of angry mountains and longing for God. And they came openhanded. They exposed my poverty of spirit as they endured more earthly poverty of their own.

The Kurds first captured me by simply inviting me to belong. This is, I believe, the radiating message of the Kurdish soul. Be welcome among us. *Belong if you will. It is an honor to us.*

It was in Kurdistan that first I heard this call. Shortly after being introduced to the Kurds in Nashville, I was invited by a relief organization to help with their work in Kurdistan. My role with this agency was always minor. Still, these early journeys into the Kurdish homeland let me experience what the Kurds of Nashville could never have made me understand. I think they knew this long before I did. I think they knew that words would fail them—even after they mastered my language—to describe their lives to one so thoroughly American. There were certainly no words they could have used to embed in me the central reality of Kurdish life—the fierce and unshakeable necessity of belonging to a people.

It was Kurdish hospitality that first hinted of this to me.

When our team visited Kurdish homes in Kurdistan or simply entered a Kurdish village, the initial welcome and ensuing hospitality was not unlike what Americans would offer returning heroes. There were no parades or hand-painted signs, of course, but there was—there is—a sheer delight in new company and a graciousness of care that seems both old world and intensely of the moment all at once.

In our work, we often found it necessary to visit people who lived in remote villages. For example, we might be required by the needs of a project to visit a man who was in charge of water or electricity in a given region. When we arrived at the man's door, we were instantly taken to the finest room in his house. Minutes into the visit, a male—a friend? a brother? a servant? We seldom knew—brought tea and then a variety of nuts, fruit, and sweets. As long as we remained in the house, food continually arrived: fresh baklava, ice cream, cookies, chocolates, or crackers. It was as though we had inadvertently signaled we were starving to death.

Our meetings were always lengthy, largely because every word passed through interpreters. Inevitably, our host's father or a village elder or some other relation would arrive. He was not intruding. He had heard their village had been honored by guests and wanted to extend a welcome.

Or, perhaps he was told that something interesting was happening at his son's house. He did not need an invitation. He belonged. He always had a place. As did perhaps a dozen other uncles, cousins, sons, or nephews.

Inevitably, one of the men would ask us to stay for dinner. Keep in mind that there were more than half a dozen in our party and our hosts had never met any of us before. There were insistences. *You must stay. We are already preparing the meat. You can smell it even now. And surely you will spend the night. In fact, there is a wedding in two days. You are welcome. It is an honor for us.*

Often the meeting moved from one house to another, from the first man's home to that of another man who would have knowledge of the matters under discussion. Again came the chai and the nuts—whatever the man had to share. You should know that these men were not bumpkins, nor were the meetings I'm describing anything like scenes from those old movies in which primitive tribes encounter Europeans for the first time and marvel at the magic of a cigarette lighter or a box of matches. Sometimes our hosts were Oxford graduates. Some had built dams, flown jets, or honed their surgical skills at Johns Hopkins. It is a mistake to assume that all Kurds are village goat herders. Far from it, as we shall see. Yet even those Kurds who had broad experience in the wider world had returned to settle again into the warm hospitality of Kurdish tradition.

I was moved by the unceasing graciousness of my Kurdish friends, but I was changed by what lay behind it. The life of nearly every Kurd I met in Kurdistan was embedded in an extended community that seemed to stretch ultimately to every place on the earth that Kurds are to be found. To my untrained eye, there was no distinguishing a man's immediate family from that of his brother or his cousin or from related clans many times removed. In fact, the word *removed* didn't seem to apply in a relational sense. Homes were open. Everyone belonged. Blood trumped every other bond.

It was impressive. We once met with a man who suddenly suggested we go ask his brother about a matter. There was no stopping it. Seven of us in two vehicles—our team, our host, two drivers, and a bodyguard—all drove the few miles to the brother's house. "Should we call first?" we suggested. "Does your brother need any warning?" "No," the man answered gently but with an unmistakable tone of scorn, as though we had made a silly and typically American suggestion.

When we arrived at the brother's house, our friend knocked once, walked in, and announced us. The quiet home instantly transformed. Tea, nuts, and fruit arrived. Soon, we could smell the beginnings of a massive meal. Women we never saw began working in the kitchen. We could hear their eager chatter. We had been there less than an hour.

Fortunately, we were able to convince the man we had to leave, but not before food was being prepared in four of his relatives' houses, beds had been assigned, and we had twice been invited to a wedding the next week.

You should stay. It is an honor for us.

I slowly began to understand something of what had allowed the Kurds to endure the horrendous seasons of their history. Each of them belonged to a system of human connections that had come before them and would survive them, something living and God-given and more important than any one of their lives at any one point in time.

And it broke my heart when I saw it, for it was from this vantage that I looked back upon the lives of the Kurds in Nashville. After being in Kurdistan, I was just able to glimpse through Kurdish eyes how isolated and individualistic American lives are. I felt for the first time a bit of the haunting loneliness that transplanted Kurds must have felt in politically free but relationally disconnected America.

In Kurdistan, a man lived as part of a people, a great roving family network devoted to near endless hospitality. By contrast, in Nashville even those who gave themselves generously to the well-being of the Kurds nevertheless set typically American limits on friendship and belonging. This was confusing and hurtful to the Kurds I knew. An expatriate Kurd would have thought nothing, for example, of spending every evening of the week visiting in the homes of his American friends. He would have hoped for picnics over the weekend and time over chai and backgammon to discuss the state of "the Kurd." This was the perpetual welcome he had known in Kurdistan.

Quite understandably, Americans expected boundaries. Appointments should be made. Times should be set. Dropping by unannounced was considered rude, and in more than one case taken as the onset of criminal activity. Even the most generous of churches might give huge sums to help immigrant Kurds and then welcome them to the standard events: a Sunday morning service, a Wednesday night Bible study, perhaps a small group gathering in a home. Yet never could these faithful have understood, much less accommodated, the kind of unending connection to other human beings that a Kurd held as both a birthright and a necessity of life.

Tragically, this meant that a Kurd eagerly welcomed to the land of plenty might find himself lost amidst the abundance and stalked by such loneliness that he struggled to retain his will to live. His well-meaning American friends would likely never know.

When I saw my beloved country and myself reflected in the mirror the Kurds held up for me, I realized how much I had to learn from them. I could never be made to despise my country, but I could be helped to see in the reflection of a more ancient culture how excess and rootlessness was making my nation—and most of Western society—shallow and aimless. The Kurds made me long for more meaningful community, for tighter connection to heritage and for a life built upon the bonds of family honor.

And I came to love them for it. I cannot tell you exactly when this began. Before they ever arrived in Nashville, I had read a bit about their history and their sufferings. My affection was likely born in those pages. Then came Asan with his heroic, haunting tales and his warrior manner. The Kurdish women of Nashville, all bright smiles and generosity—especially with food—won me too. Then came my uniquely Kurdish tutoring in belonging.

Yet, this odd love for a foreign people also grew from a thousand kindnesses and from the poetry of Kurdish ways.

I loved them when I was giving a talk about democracy on Kurdish television and the interpreter, a dear man named Hashim Sushi, became so moved that he started kissing me profusely right there on live TV.

I loved them when news that a Nashville aid worker's wife was sick reached the Kurdish community and a dozen of them showed up at the man's house with food enough to feed a village.

I loved them for loving the United States despite the wrongs my country has done them. I loved, also, their gratitude for the good.

I loved them when I was in Kurdistan and my Sharp Wizard—a granddaddy of smart phones and tablets—was stolen. I returned to Kurdistan six months later to find Hashim Sushi, the thief, and my Wizard—carried in an oily farm sack—at my hotel room door. The thief was expected to apologize. I was expected to forgive. Both of us were under threat from the 5'2" Hashim. "It would be a shame for us," he said, as though announcing the meaning of life.

I could not keep from loving them when gunfire broke out at a stadium event in Kurdistan and three Kurds jumped on me to protect me. I had been in their homes. They took this to mean that they had a covenantal responsibility for me. And bullets were flying.

I love them, too, for what they are showing the world now. The supposedly backwards, tribal Kurds—persecuted and despised for generations—are demonstrating that their time has come.

And I love them because if there are any people who might move to the far side of the world because their children love a song—or to heal the "Aky, Aky Hartz" of their loved ones—it would be the Kurds.

CHAPTER 4

A KURDISH TALE

"The Kurds are homeless even at home, and
stateless abroad. Their ancient woes are locked
inside an obscure language. They have powerful,
impatient enemies and a few rather easily bored friends.
Their traditional society is considered
a nuisance at worst and a curiosity at best.
For them the act of survival, even identity itself,
is a kind of victory."

—Christopher Hitchens[1]

When I think back over my years in friendship with Kurds, what usually returns to my memory most forcefully are my long conversations with groups of Kurdish men. Usually late at night, and over cups of tea and handfuls of pistachio nuts, fierce Kurdish warriors— for most all Kurdish men are fierce Kurdish warriors— pressed the case of their people upon me.

I had never heard such voices, nor had I ever been spoken to with such fire by someone not intending me harm. I often thought during these hours that if my non-Kurdish friends at home happened upon the scene they would rush to my rescue thinking I was in danger. A Kurd, in fact most men in the Middle East, can speak with such passion and volume, with such waving of the arms and piercing intensity, that it requires a certain presence of mind not to take offense.

During one conversation, an older man began to raise his arms above his head and shout at me in one of the more biting Kurdish languages. It stunned me a bit. I did not understand what he was saying—my interpreter had temporarily left the room—but I thought he must be taking me to task for some misdeed by the American government. It turned out he was simply describing the follies of Ottoman petroleum policy—more than a century ago. Such are the passions of the Kurds.

On another occasion, several American friends and I were sitting with some of the valiant Kurdish Peshmerga one evening. Each of these warriors had Kalashnikov machine guns resting on their laps or at their sides. As one man became increasingly animated, he grabbed his gun in both hands and began shaking it just above his lap as he spoke. Though I knew it wasn't true, his movements were perfectly suited to the words "If you don't leave my country, I will kill you and all you love." One of our group wrote down these words in his journal in an attempt to capture the feel of the moment: "You see this gun! I can use it! I've killed many people! I will kill you too! You get it?" The man was actually welcoming us: "You are welcome here. And we will defend you with our lives, our new American friends. Thank you for honoring us." There were times I was desperate for my interpreter to catch up to what a speaker was saying. Until he did, I occasionally thought my life might be at risk.

These were among my favorite times among the Kurds, though, and only after some years did I come to understand why. It was when I realized what was always in the room with us. It was Kurdish history. It was the power of the Kurds as a people through time. My Kurdish hosts knew that I did not know, that we Americans did not understand, who they were and how great they had been. It frustrated them. When this was combined with the injustices of their history and their serial betrayals, the combustion of it all was nearly too much. The shouting and the arm waving began as though an offense of 1914 had taken place only the day before, as though something could still be done to fix it all if only we Americans would learn a little history.

I was often moved by how much every detail, every claim, meant to the Kurds I knew. During one conversation that took place during a long, hot drive, two English-speaking Kurds in my vehicle took great pains over many hours to convince me that the famed Arabian horse was originally a Kurdish horse. The Arabs had stolen the memory of Kurdish horsemanship as well as the great symbol of the horse itself. This then led to an angry rant about how the Arabs had also remade the great Saladin into an Arab. There were actual tears of anger over this.

Then the conversation turned to religion. The one Kurdish Christian in our vehicle declared that he could never be a Muslim because it was a religion of being Arab. I expected violence any moment. Everyone in the vehicle was armed but me. Instead, the Muslim among us simply said, "Well, I want to be a Muslim, but I do not want to be an Arab Muslim." This made the Christian laugh so hard that everyone laughed with him, the Muslim included. "There is only Arab Islam. What are you talking?! Listen to him. He wants Kurdish Islam only. What a guy!" I was deeply relieved for the Kurdish graciousness, but I remember wondering what it was like to be part of a people with a constant claim of injustice against the wider world.

I must admit that the Kurds changed my understanding of history. On no subject was this so much the case as on the subject of Iraq. To most of the world, the Kurds are a people group who belong to Iraq, that troubled, culturally divided nation recently liberated by a coalition of armies. The usual assumption is that now, after this liberation, the Kurds can take their destined place as loyal citizens of Iraq and, over time, allow their Kurdishness to drift away as they become ever more—"Iraqi."

Iraq—the nation, the overarching state, the structure imposed—is ultimate, in this way of thinking. It is the inevitable destination, the proper arrangement, the way of things. It is the insistence of history. Iraq has always been. It is as natural and original as any of the great empires of the ancient world. Always, the Kurds are expected to be Iraqis before they are Kurds, and, presumably, instead of being Kurds.

The Kurds, though, do not agree and this is the reason much of the Middle East finds them an offense. The Kurds wish always and above all things simply to be Kurds. It would not seem too much to ask, but it is a transgression in our collective age, a time when a people like the Kurds only gain meaning in the eyes of the world by belonging to a larger, more acceptable group. Yet, the Kurds do not wish to belong, except to themselves. This makes them a threat to artificial monarchies and plans for a new world order, to dictators in Baghdad and dictatorial benevolence crafted in the capitals of the world.

The Kurds know—and never for a moment forget— what most people in the world have never understood. The nation of Iraq is not a centuries-old country with natural boundaries and an organically blended population. Instead, Iraq is a structure of artificial boundaries and unnaturally combined tribes and religions conceived by Europeans just after World War I.

Perhaps it was the best idea suggested at the time. Great minds and noble hearts gave birth to the nation of Iraq, Winston Churchill, Gertrude Bell, and T. E. Lawrence among them. There was no intention of torturing history with an unworkable state of affairs.

Yet there was a certain high-handedness about the conferences and policies that refashioned the Middle East in that era—not surprising, I suppose, after the defeat of a four-hundred-year-old Ottoman Empire at great cost in lives. Winston Churchill gave voice to this imperiousness when he later boasted, "I created Transjordan with a stroke of a pen on a Sunday afternoon in Cairo."[2]

There was much the same attitude—though a bit more discussion—surrounding the creation of modern Iraq. The name was not new. It had been used since the sixth century. It was probably a derivative of the name for the ancient city of Uruk, which we read in our Bibles as "Erech."[3] The word evolved into a name for the region as a whole. In fact, ask most Arabs what the word *Iraq* means and they will tell you something akin to "fertile," "abundant," "well-watered," or "lush." This describes most all of the Fertile Crescent, the land between the Tigris and Euphrates—the word *Mesopotamia* means "land between two rivers"—which our textbooks tell us is the "cradle of civilization."

At the end of the Great War, Europeans assumed responsibility for the lands once ruled by the Ottoman Empire. England was made responsible—given a "mandate," in the language of the time—for the region that is generally Iraq today. No matter how England chose to fulfill its mandate, however, it was bound to disappoint the tribes, ethnicities, and religions that lived under its rule. The victorious Europeans had simply promised too much after the war.

Moved by mostly noble intentions, they had declared the right of "self-determination" for all peoples. At a peace conference in Paris, they authored a Treaty of Sevres which—reflecting Woodrow Wilson's insistence that "nationalities which are now under Turkish rule should be assured an undoubted security of life and an absolutely unmolested opportunity of autonomous development"—mentioned the Kurds specifically as due for a nation of their own.

These lofty promises could not overcome the complexities of the Arab world and dreams ignited by oil. The Treaty of Sevres was soon abandoned in favor of a Treaty of Lausanne, which revoked the promise of Kurdish autonomy. Instead, the Kurds found themselves bundled together with Arab tribes (the Kurds are not Arabs) and with Shi'ite Muslims (the majority of Kurds are Sunni Muslims) and placed under an Arab, Hashemite king by the name of Faisal. As though to guarantee discord, the Europeans left undefined the exact border between the new Turkish Republic and the new nation of Iraq. This would prove an expensive error.

There were many errors. Among the worst of them has been that since the nation of Iraq sprang fully formed from European imaginations in the early 1920s, the world has expected the Kurds to be Iraqis. It does not seem to matter that the Kurds were already an ancient people centuries before Rome was an empire. It does not seem to matter that the world once promised the Kurds a homeland of their own. It does not seem to matter that an Iraqi regime has warred against the Kurds almost from the moment Iraq became a nation. None of this deters the nations of the world from insisting the Kurds be good Iraqis and live obediently under a regime that despises them.

My Kurdish friends would weep as they recounted the injustice of Iraq and I slowly began to feel some of their agony. One evening, after a late evening meal at a Kurdish restaurant in Nashville—my family out of town and the night unclaimed—I asked the owner, a dear friend, to take whatever time he needed to teach me what Kurds most wanted Americans to understand about their past. He agreed.

"It begins," he said quietly, "with the land . . ." The two hours that followed were transforming for me.

Before there were human designs and animosities to leave their mark, there was simply the land. It seemed to be waiting for the Kurds. It was a region wrapped by two mountain ranges that surged from plateaus and plains as though already defying encroachment from the outer world. It was a magnificent and daunting landscape, so rugged it was fit only for a people who would dwell in its embrace as if it were the embrace of God. The Kurds were such a people and it has done much to make them who they are. "Geography is destiny," wrote historian David McCullough. He was thinking of American history when he penned these words, but they could adorn the banner over the story of the Kurds as well.

For a Kurd, this geography has only one name: Kurdistan, which literally means, "the place of the Kurds." Not "northern Iraq." Not some expediency of an Ottoman Empire or a League of Nations or a United Nations coalition. No. Kurdistan. Where mankind was born and the mountains safeguard the righteous and no invader lasts. Where the eyes of children are windows to eternity and the ways of the Medes and the Persians are still to be found. Where even that man of God, Abraham, was willing to end his journey, thinking this Kurdistan must be the Promised Land.

This is the Kurdish homeland, the object of their poetry, the mistress of their songs, the memorial of their dead, the monument to their injustices and the embodiment of their dreams of nationhood. It is perched at the north end of Mesopotamia, pillared by the magnificent Zagros and Taurus Mountains and carved by running water as though intended for a tribal, village-bound people.

Some say it takes these mountains to make a Kurd. Most Kurds have heard their fathers say, "Always, we have the mountains." Most have heard the stories, or perhaps were there, when the mountains were the only place to go, when the armies of monsters crossed the borders, and the gunships and the gas canisters came. Even in peace, Kurds look to the mountains with gratitude, remembering. As Middle East expert David McDowell has written, "Although an increasing proportion of Kurds leave the mountain valleys to live in towns or cities, the mountain image loses nothing of its potency, for nations are built in the imagination before they are built on the ground."[4]

The Kurdish motto is often reported as "We have no friends." The Kurds themselves are more likely to say, "We have no friends but the mountains." This better expresses the great truth of Kurdish history: the mountains belong to the people and the people belong to the mountains. These mountains—*their* mountains—are not just geographical features. They are refuge. They are defender. They are, in a sense that only the Kurds truly understand, father to the people.

A popular movie, entitled *A Season in Hakkari,* so perfectly captured this connection between the Kurds and their mountains that Turkish censors—eager to silence any celebration of the Kurdish spirit—banned the film as a threat to their state. The most offending scene, apparently, was one in which a fairy tale explains how the Kurds came to their mountains.

When Allah was creating these mountains, the mountains cried, they cried a lot. They said, "Who's going to take care of us? You are making us so snowy and so void." The mountains said "Nobody will come." Then Allah showed the Kurds to them. He said, "These are desperate, they've got no cure. They'll stay and take care of you." The mountains waited and the mountains cried. And thus we've landed on these mountains.

It is a typically Kurdish story. The mountains are forlorn. The Kurds are "desperate" and without "cure." All is the will of Allah. Yet these words so resonate with Kurds today that many have memorized them and taken their meaning to heart.

This, then, is where the Kurdish story begins. Not with empires and kingdoms, but with the imprint of the land upon a people, with mountains and surging streams and arcing plains absorbed into a common soul. It explains an oddity among modern Kurds. An expatriate Kurd in Geneva or Detroit, asked about the source of their sadness, might very well answer, "I miss my mountains," even though they have never been to Kurdistan before. They are referring not to specific rock formations at the north end of the Fertile Crescent. They are referring to a mystical Kurdistan, to whose mountains all Kurds belong.

It was from this spectacular stage that the Kurds first stepped into the pages of history. Scholars debate the exact moment it occurred. Some argue it was around 3,000 BC in a Sumerian document that described a "land of Kardo." Others contend that this appearing came four centuries before Christ when Xenophon recorded that retreating Greeks were harassed by "Kardouchoi" who "dwelt up among the mountains ... a warlike people ... not subjects of the King." Some scholars, though, insist that we are uncertain of any reference until the Seljuk Turks began using "Kurdistan" as a geographical term in the twelfth century.

These debates will never end. Far more important to the Kurds is their unshakeable belief that they are the descendants of the ancient Medes. This belief, more than any other, defines their sense of community, their pride, their ethics, their warrior code, their religious identity, and their insistence upon a place of their own among the nations of the world.

It is the claim the Kurds make most often of themselves. The Kurdish television channel broadcast from Europe is named Medya TV. The Kurdish national anthem contains the line "We are the children of the Medes." A famous and beloved Kurdish patriotic poem, entitled "Who Am I?" and written by the revered poet, Cigerxwîn, also makes this declaration.[5]

Who am I, you ask?
The Kurd of Kurdistan . . .
I am the valiant fighter of the mountains
Who is not in love with death
But for the sake of life and freedom
He sacrifices himself,
So the land of his ancestors,
The invincible Medes,
His beloved Kurdistan,
May be unchained.

As with much that involves the Kurds, this claim about the Medes is surrounded by intense scholarly debate. Kurdish scholars, of course, insist upon it. Some eminent linguists and historians support them. Others refuse to believe there can be any linear connection between a people as ancient as eight hundred years before the time of Christ and the Kurds today. It is an important and fascinating topic, far too bound up in scholarly debate and esoteric knowledge for the layman to decide.

It may not matter. The Kurds have already decided the issue for themselves. A casual walk through most any Kurdish town will reveal Mede restaurants, Mede schools, Mede tea shops, Mede clothing stores and Mede football clubs. Popular songs by Kurdish singer/songwriter Şivan Perwer send Kurdish audiences into frenzies when they invoke the Medes. Political speeches routinely extol "Our fathers, the Medes," and Kurdish children are schooled in the certainty that their ancestors were the architects of a mighty and ancient Empire.

Even Kurdish scholars recognize, though, this may be an attempt to overcorrect one of the great problems of Kurdish history. As a professor in Erbil who asked not to be named told me, "The Kurds are the 'also-rans' of history. We are there, but we have no separate history. We are always part of other nations and our contributions are always attributed to other nations. We are indistinguishable from other nations. Some of the great figures of history—Cyrus the Great or Cyaxares or Darius or Saladin—all are Kurds but all are remembered as belonging to other peoples."

This is an observation that plays heavily on the minds of thinking Kurds, one that has been used against them often by their enemies. *The Kurds are not a people. They are a loose band of unaffiliated tribes.*

The truth is that the Kurds did not emerge as a unified people until after World War I. From the days of the ancient Median Empire until the end of the Great War, the Kurds surfaced from time to time in the pages of history, like sea creatures appearing momentarily above the surface of the deep. As late as 1874, explorers spoke of Kurdistan as being among the world's "uncivilized lands." There were Kurdish tribes, fiefdoms and miniature kingdoms, but there was no nation or people group in any sense the outer world understood.

Nevertheless, they were there. During all those centuries when little was written about them, they were building their villages, extending their familial reach, worshipping their God and repelling an unending line of invaders. They clung to their mountains and their traditional ways, bickered with other tribes and won an awe-inspiring reputation as horsemen and warriors. Yet they were not prominent in the kind of events history bothers to notice until a modern war forced the modern world to pay attention.

This ignorance of the Kurdish journey through time was unfortunate and, eventually, tragic. Their region was mentioned by Strabo, Herodotus, Polybius, and Pliny. If the Medes are even remotely their ancestors, then on the streets of Zakho, Diyarbakir, Erbil, Mosul, and Kirkuk today walk men in whom flow the blood of warriors who impressed Assyrian kings like Shalmaneser III, Sargon the Great, and Sennacherib. Allied with the Babylonians, they ended the Assyrian Empire and later ruled an empire of their own, the size of which would today cover Iran, Iraq, and eastern Turkey. They were conquered by the Persians, but then joined their conquerors in ruling over a Medo-Persian Empire that is remembered for delivering the Israelites from their Babylonian captivity, and for laws and customs that shape Western culture to this day.

The history recounted in the Bible also includes the Kurds. They were present at the time of the prophet Daniel and many would have converted to his God. Others would have witnessed the ascent of a woman named Esther to the side of Ahasuerus, King of the Persians. Centuries later, the ancestors of the Kurds were witnesses in Jerusalem when the Christian Church was born on the Day of Pentecost. The Greek historian Luke specifically notes that among the many nationalities that saw the commotion of that day were "Parthians and Medes and Elamites and the dwellers in Mesopotamia."[6]

The "Magi from the East" who are part of the story of Christ's birth also have influence upon the Kurd's Median heritage. From about 200 BC until the birth of Christianity, the religion of the Medes was primarily Zoroastrianism. Its priests were Magi, a term taken from the Persian word, *meguceen*, which means "fire worshipper." Our English word "magician" originates from the name for these priests, who were similar to wizards or enchanters and who used astrology to understand the universe. It is not hard to understand why the Kurds would be eager to claim for their heritage the religious seekers who were among the first worshippers of Jesus Christ.

Many other Kurdish worshippers of Jesus would come afterward. Christianity entered the Kurdish lands soon after the birth of the Church, largely through the ministry of the apostle Thomas. Two missionaries, Addai and Mari, followed Thomas and left in their wake a thriving Christian community that eventually spread throughout the region. This continued for centuries until the birth of Islam, which in 634 AD became the dominant and official religion of the Kurdish dominions.

For nearly a millennium afterward, the Kurds lived as a largely Muslim people, ruled by a succession of caliphs, ever confirming their historic reputation as skilled fighters from the mountains. The currents of history would not leave them to their own. Through Kurdistan trekked Muslim armies bent upon the destruction of Byzantium, the Christian empire of the east centered in Constantinople. Traders also passed through Kurdistan during these centuries, the possibilities of which were not lost on the Kurds themselves. For much of this time, the word *Kurd* was interchangeable with the word *brigand,* the tribes of

Kurdistan apparently having learned to help themselves to the wealth passing by their door.

At around 1500 AD, two events shoved the thriving, prosperous Kurds into centuries of decline. Oddly, the first of these devastations is celebrated by Europeans to this day as one of the great strides forward in the progress of mankind. In 1487, Vasco da Gama sailed around the Cape of Good Hope, proving that sea travel was possible from Europe around Africa to the Far East. Trade between Europe and the Orient began moving by ships on oceans rather than by caravans through the Kurdish realms. So shattering was this shift for the Kurds that one historian calls 1487 a "calamitous date" after which "Kurdistan quickly became a mountainous irrelevancy."[7]

The second decimating event was the conflict between the Persian and the Ottoman Empires. Since the Kurds were ethnically related to Persia, they supported its armies and found themselves at the center of a centuries-long war. Deportations, battles that leveled village after village, and religious upheavals exacerbated the troubles of the already impoverished Kurds and left them a broken, humiliated people. "Kurdistan sank into a dubious kind of peace," an historian writes, "more like the peace of a wilderness."[8]

Hope of Kurdistan's restoration came during the 1800s and from an unexpected source. A nine-year war between Russia and Persia ended with an agreement that placed some Kurdish dominions under the control of the Russian Empire. This meant that the backwards, poverty-stricken, dispirited Kurds came under the influence of a European empire with new ideas, new technologies, and access to the markets of the world. Kurdistan began to rise. Its ruling class sent its young to European universities. Liberal concepts of religious tolerance prevailed and visions of ethnic nationalism began to stir hopes of a prosperous and independent Kurdistan.

In one of the great tragedies of Kurdish history, it was just when all the forces that might have meant nationhood were working in Kurdistan's favor that she underwent a near-complete religious implosion. In the mid-1800s, inexplicable religious fanaticism turned the Kurds from a religiously tolerant people to religious insanity. Bloodbaths followed. One notable massacre took five thousand lives. Sunni Muslims turned on Shi'ite Muslims and Christians turned on Jews. A surely insane tribal chief drank the blood of a rival patriarch. Another committed atrocities that are among the bloodiest in history.

The timing could not have been worse. At the end of World War I and with the end of the Ottoman Empire, rather than a strong, progressive, Western-leaning Kurdistan, a small, splintered, religion-crazed people were all the victorious Europeans could see. In their shattered condition, the Kurds were not a people to whom Western powers would give independence. They were not a people to whom the Great War's victors owed even the keeping of a promise. "Kurdistan was a land," contends one writer, "with its infrastructure wrecked, its society in utter disarray, its intelligentsia dispersed, and the tribal chieftains and sheiks in full control of what was left."[9]

This was the tragic moment that gave birth to all the tragedies yet to befall the Kurds. There would be no nation. Squabbling mullahs and village elders could not be entrusted with that power. Instead, there would be an Iraq and the Kurds would be cobbled into it. A monarchy that could not rule would give way to revolutionaries who could not lead and would ultimately surrender to a madman who would not yield to any moral restraint.

The Kurds would be savaged by it all.

The betrayal of the Kurds after World War I and the attempt to extinguish them into a monolithic Iraq led to many of the more familiar agonies of Kurdish history. Despising them for their unceasing resistance, Turkey persecuted the Kurds for decades. Official documents referred to the Kurds as "mountain Turks," thus refusing to acknowledge the distinct Kurdish heritage. All things Kurdish were banned. Though today this has ceased to be law, it is still custom. I once made the mistake of saying the word *Kurdistan* too loudly on an Istanbul street and soon found myself being questioned by an overhearing policeman. This was well after the dawn of the new millennium.

Iraq's monarchy often assaulted the Kurds for the same reason the Turks had: they would not conform. Then came the Baathists, oppressive socialists not unlike the Nazis of World War II, and with them Saddam Hussein. Though he dressed in Kurdish clothing for the watching world and appointed a smattering of Kurds to government positions merely for show, Saddam Hussein became to the Kurds what Adolf Hitler was to the Jews of Europe: The Annihilator.

Yet, oddly, it may be the Great Evil of Saddam that prevents outsiders from knowing what Kurds would have us know of their greatness through the centuries. As my restaurant owner friend wound down on that cool Nashville night, he said with the sadness of centuries, "We were a great and a respected people. We could have become a mighty nation, a prosperous nation. All the world knows now is the Kurd as a victim, the Kurd in exile, the Kurd as the people with no home, no land, and no place of their own. It is a shame to us."

I was forever changed by that late night tutoring at my friend's restaurant. By that time, I had earned a doctorate in history. I knew much of the history my friend recounted, but I knew it as just that: "history." Something past. Something remote. Something I required a book and a professor to press upon me. I never felt involved in that history. It was what European victors and Middle Eastern competitor nations had once done to Kurds on the other side of the world and long before I was born.

My Kurdish friends, though, had heard these complaints at their mothers' breasts. Their fathers had wept at mealtimes over the injustices suffered by great-grandfathers. Kurdish men swore oaths of vengeance for offenses decades old. Such was the white heat a Kurd might feel for his people's past.

I could only hope to understand by comparing it to a shameful stream in my own past. For many generations there were vicious racists in my family line. Some of my ancestors were members of the Ku Klux Klan. Some were outspoken activists against the rights of southern blacks. One of my great-uncles shot a black man just for walking in his yard. My grandparents thought nothing of announcing proudly at a family breakfast that they had successfully locked blacks out of their Methodist church in Albany, Georgia.

I was stunned. And ashamed. Growing up as the son of an Army officer, I could not imagine my life without my black friends—or my Hispanic, Asian, and whatever friends. I had never witnessed such hatred and here it was spewing from my own grandparents and at my mother's breakfast table.

My utter disgust with this part of my heritage marked me and I've set my life toward the goal of ending its evil legacy.

I can compare this to the thinking of my Kurdish friends only by reversing my heritage in my imagination. Were I not a white descendant of racists, but rather the son and grandson of those who suffered Jim Crow laws and escaped lynchings, who were beaten at lunch counters and shut out of voting booths, I would feel quite differently. What rage, what fierce determination to right these wrongs might fill me? What fire would possess me after knowing of my grandfather's humiliation, my uncle's murder, or the schools, jobs, and basic civil rights denied to my mother? I would have to fight daily against a deforming bitterness.

This is why much of what I learned about Kurdish history made me fear for my Kurdish friends. What would it mean to them, their souls and the souls of their children, to believe themselves hated and accursed the world over? How would they ever recover if the meaning of the phrase "a people without a friend" pressed itself unchangeably into the Kurds' view of themselves? Could they ever rise above their longstanding curse?

The first hint of answers to these questions came to me on a Sunday afternoon in Nashville and, again, at a restaurant. I was finishing a late lunch at the International Market on Nolensville Road. My friend Mezgeen Zbari had started the Market years before, but had since returned to Kurdistan. I missed him and thought of him as I finished my *shish* alone.

A handful of Kurdish teenage boys were finishing their meal at the same time and making plans, as teenagers will, with the kind of attention to detail typical of the British High Command. The teens were likely just planning to attend a movie. Whatever they intended, their strategy involved leaving one of their number behind, whose job was apparently to stare at this cell phone until further instructions arrived.

He was being obedient when two policemen walked through the doors. The officers went to the counter, ordered their gyros and drink, and conversed while the food was being prepared. I noticed the Kurdish boy shrink. He would have crawled into the napkin dispenser had he been able. The policemen terrified him. Moments later, the two officers paid for their food and turned to leave. Before they did, one of them nodded to the young Kurd and said, "Hey, buddy" in the deepest of Tennessee accents. Then they were gone.

The young man—I learned later his name was Adel— cut his eyes to me with some embarrassment. He knew I had seen.

I smiled. "They are not Mukhabarat!" I said this as kindly as I could, trying to be encouraging. I thought using the word for the Iraqi secret police might show him I understood. It didn't.

"What?" he said, blank-faced.

"They are not Nazis," I said, attempting another smile. "I noticed they made you nervous."

"Yeah. I got pushed around by some cops last week. I just want them to stay away from me."

"Sorry to hear that. I've heard Nashville police are pretty decent." I wished later I hadn't said this. I didn't mean to challenge him. But, well, it was true.

"Maybe." He shrugged and looked out the windows. "But they hate Kurds. It's a bitch being a Kurd."

I nodded my head as though I understood. I was trying to decide if he was sincere.

"I'd love to be a Kurd," I found myself saying. It wasn't exactly true, but I was moved to say it by the look on Adel's face. I would be delighted to be a Kurd, of course, but since I believe God determines these things, I don't walk around wishing to be other than I am.

"You would love to be a Kurd?" He asked this with as much incredulous scorn as I have ever heard poured into so few words.

"Yep. In fact, some of my biggest heroes are Kurds." I had started this and there was no retreat.

He stared at me in disbelieving silence. "Name one," he challenged.

"Mustafa Barzani."

He said nothing, but smirked a bit as though my first choice was too obvious. I had named the George Washington of Kurdistan. It was too easy. Adel was wearing a Ziggy Marley t-shirt and a trucker's cap adorned with a sexually exaggerated cartoon blond. Perhaps I had blown my lead.

I decided to lean in. "Saladin—greatest Kurd ever. Jalal Talabani—president of Iraq. Nazar Ahmad—champion bodybuilder. Bahman Ghobadi—famous director."

He smiled slightly. He knew I had been waiting for him.

"Okay. Okay." He said with mock resignation, trying to shut me down.

"Mezgeen Zbari—greatest man in the world.'

"Who's *that?*" he asked, and it pleased me he was listening.

"Founder of this restaurant. Maker of this baklava."

He laughed. "No fair!"

"My rules," I said, looking at him sideways.

There was silence. He was thinking. His phone went off. He read the text and said, "I gotta go."

"Alright. Good talkin' to ya."

A slight hesitation as he started to leave made me think there was something more to say.

"Hey," I said to hold him at door. "The Kurds are about to amaze everyone in the world. Don't forget who you are." I knew this sounded like a line from *The Lion King*, but I had to take my shot.

"Yeah. I won't." He was sincere. It made me hope there had been a connection.

Then, just as he pushed through the door, he said, "I think us Kurds are about to kick ass." He put so much emphasis on the last two words it made me laugh.

And I knew it was true. History, their history, was finally turning in their favor. It meant the world to me at the time that a fourteen-year-old Kurd in Nashville knew it too.

Fathers of Modern Kurdistan

MASSOUD BARZANI

His father was the legendary Mullah Mustafa Barzani. He was born in the short-lived Mahabad Republic, one of the most courageous attempts to achieve a Kurdish homeland. He is the head of the Kurdistan Democratic Party, the head of the Kurdistan Regional Government, and has been, for much of his life, at the head of resistance to the evils of Saddam Hussein. Massoud Barzani, a quiet, diminutive man, has gone beyond merely continuing the work of his father. He has become a Kurdish hero in his own right.

Born on August 16, 1946, he assumed the lead of the Kurdistan Democratic Party (KDP) in 1979 upon the death of his father. If Mustafa was the revolutionary spirit, Massoud is a wise builder of free Kurdistan. Tempered in exile, in a costly civil war, and through decades of Baghdad's murderous policies, he has moved beyond the thinking of a war leader and has helped to lay the foundation of the modern Kurdish Miracle.

He prepared the way for free elections in Kurdistan within months of securing control of the government in 1992. He became the global face of Kurdistan through his wide travels on behalf of the Kurdish cause and his high-profile meetings with George W. Bush, Tony Blair, Italian Prime Minister Berlusconi, King Abdullah of Saudi Arabia, and King Abdullah of Jordan. He has been honored by the Pope for offering persecuted Christians of the Middle East a safe haven in Kurdistan. He has also shown great wisdom in resisting the encroachments of a corrupt and unstable government in Baghdad and in establishing Kurdistan as an independent economic region and a valuable trading partner to neighboring countries.

Massoud Barzani heads one of the ruling tribes of Kurdistan, the very kind of vast and wealthy clan that will have to release power in the years to come for the nation to be truly free. If his past actions are any indication, he will likely lead his country and his tribe toward whatever is best for the Kurds of future generations. A U.S. diplomat once made the mistake of introducing Massoud almost exclusively as the son of the great man, Mullah Mustafa Barzani. A Kurdish leader corrected him. "He not merely the son of Mullah Mustafa. He is a son of Kurdistan. That is what you must know about him."

CHAPTER 5

SOLECKI'S COMPLAINT

"I was impressed at how the Kurds make the best of hopeless situations. They are tough and adaptable, which is perhaps the key to their longevity in this war-ravaged region."

—Christopher Hitchens[1]

There is a sweet story about the Kurds that has returned to me again and again through the years. It comes to my mind whenever I think about the innocence and openness I often felt in Kurdistan.

You should know I am not blindly sentimental about the Kurds as Americans often can be about people from other lands. We tend to have movie images playing in our heads. We want our Irishmen dancing and waving shillelaghs. We want our Germans wearing monocles, hoisting beer steins, and dressed in leather shorts. We tend to live in Disney World.

I understand that there is evil in the world and that the Kurds are not immune to it. I've witnessed the same vile deeds committed by Kurds as are committed by every tribe on earth. We all live somewhere between the better angels of our nature and the pull of the dark and the demonic, between the part of us we give to God and the part the Prince of Darkness seems to own. Kurds are no different. They will tell you the same.

Still, my experiences among the Kurds have left me convinced that some combination of simplicity, devotion, and honor distinguishes them at their core. Or at least it does when they allow. This is the reason I think of one particular story when I think of the Kurds at their best.

Though it may be difficult to believe, there was a time when Muslims and Jews lived peacefully side-by-side. They still do in some parts of the world, but it is rare. It was common, though, in the villages of Kurdistan at one time and no one ever thought it odd. We are more accustomed to inhumanity between religions now, particularly between Muslims and Jews, but it was not always so.

From their unique history, the majority of Kurds have acquired different attitudes towards the Jews than most Muslims. In fact, a significant number of Kurds are Jews. This has come about in a variety of ways, but the most interesting to me has to do with the exile of the ancient Jews in Babylon.

When the mighty Babylonian Empire conquered Assyria, it then swarmed into Israel and took its people into exile. The descendants of Abraham thus became slaves to Babylonian kings with names like Nebuchadnezzar II and Amel-Marduk. The pleading tone of Psalm 137 expresses the confused sadness of these exiles:

By the rivers of Babylon we sat and wept
When we remembered Zion....
Our tormentors demanded songs of joy...
How can we sing the Lord's songs in a foreign land

In time, the Medo/Persian Empire conquered Babylon and permitted the Jews to return to their land. This is the backstory of Old Testament books like Ezra and Nehemiah. We know, though, that some of the Jews, perhaps the majority, chose to remain where they were rather than return to the land of their fathers. This meant that they lived in an empire ruled, in part, by the ancestors of the Kurds. My Kurdish friends insist that this led to two dramatic results. First, it meant that a prosperous and respected Jewish community arose in the heart of Persia and left a legacy of Kurdish Judaism that has survived to this day. Second, this favor between Jews and Medes/Persians continued through the generations, even into the age of Islam.

It is this favor that is at the heart of the Kurdish story I love most. It is best understood if we picture a Kurdish village sometime in the 1940s. The previous years have been difficult but the people survive. The village endures, and it endures with Jews and Muslims living together. A mosque and a synagogue adorn the village, with members of both faiths sitting on the town councils and cooperating on nearly every aspect of village life. No one thinks it strange.

Still, it is the mid-1940s and a world war is just drawing to an end. That war has been, in part, about Jews. A movement to create a Jewish homeland has arisen. Its leaders declare that Jews should have a homeland of their own, so they never suffer the ghettoes and the concentration camps again. Our villagers watch these events unfold and try to understand. There is much discussion, much wondering at the meaning of it all.

The year 1948 arrives and an astonishing thing has occurred. The new nation of Israel has been born. Jews are streaming to Israel from all over the world. In the Kurdish villages where Jews and Muslims have lived together for decades, the Jews begin to wonder if they, too, should leave for a new life in a nation of their own.

More than a new homeland compels them. For many years, despite the warmth they share with their Muslim neighbors, the Jews have been increasingly oppressed by the government in Baghdad. In 1934, the state began restricting the Jews' freedom to travel. In 1935, Baghdad instituted quotas for Jews in the secondary schools and universities. In 1936, Jews were required to have a Muslim business partner in order to own a business. Even worse, in 1939, Baghdad required a pro-Nazi curriculum in the nation's schools. Though in 1948 no one knew it was coming, the 1950s would witness Iraq's Jews being stripped of all rights of citizenship. It had not happened yet, but it was the drift of an increasingly anti-Semitic Iraqi state and the Jews of the world were no longer willing to sit quietly and let a murderous tide turn against them.

No, hard as it would be, the Kurdish Jews would have to leave their Muslim friends.

The news is devastating to the Muslim villagers. With these Jews at their side they have survived life in an unforgiving land, built together and mourned each other's dead. Now, their Jewish neighbors—who in some villages are more than half the population—are leaving. Forever.

When the day of departure comes, the Muslims force gifts and food for the journey upon their friends and walk with them as far as they can. Then comes the final embrace and grief that will not end for years.

There is little unique about this story thus far. Farewell scenes such as this were likely repeated the world over after the creation of Israel in 1948.

What distinguishes this story is what came after the Jews departed. Many of the Muslims who remained in the villages did not merely grieve the loss of their friends for a season and then allow their memories and their affections to fade. It would have been perfectly understandable if they had, but this was not what they chose.

Instead, the Muslim villagers decided to honor the Jews they would never see again. They would do it, they declared, by maintaining the synagogue. This was the decision in dozens of Kurdish villages. Lovingly, the Muslims set themselves to sweeping the floors, repairing the roofs and replacing the loose stones of synagogues no one would ever use. They also lit candles on holy days and occasionally gathered to sing songs their Jewish friends had taught them.

It is a moving story, this memory of Muslims tending synagogues to honor their absent Jewish friends. They knew the Jews would never return. They knew the synagogues would always remain empty. Still, they swept and repaired and remembered.

Had they done this for as little as half a year, the story would lose none of its force. We know, though, that some villages maintained empty synagogues for years—even decades. I have spoken to Muslim men in Kurdistan who remembered caring for empty synagogues at their fathers' sides. Most of them said it would have seemed strange had it happened any other way.

I do not want to make too much of this story. It would likely not be the same today. Still, this bit of history is a symbol of what is to me the most endearing characteristic of the Kurds: they constantly surprise the non-Kurdish world by living their lives with a determined difference, as though they intend to take what life grants them and rework it until it is uniquely theirs.

This was a theme of much that the Kurds taught me about themselves. "We are not as you think," I would hear again and again. "We have not become like the others." By this phrase, "the others," they meant a variety of things: other Muslims, other people of the Middle East, the others fighting in this war, even the others who have come from the Middle East to live in America. The Kurds I knew emphasized this so much that I soon realized they were wrestling with this matter of their "difference" themselves, as though they were rediscovering it after a long season of loss.

I was deeply mystified by this constant grappling with their differences until I understood it as part of the Kurdish Moment just then unfolding. The truth is that when I first began to know the Kurds, there was already a "Great Thaw" taking place. The Kurds I knew were starting to come back to themselves. For so many crushing years, they and their kinsmen had lived as a despised, hunted, betrayed people. Every expression of their heritage, any line of a poem or note of a song that celebrated who they truly were, was banned and its creator punished. Kurds were slaughtered simply for being Kurds. In fact, being a Kurd itself had been a crime in parts of the world, something to be punished. No wonder they shut down, as individuals and as a culture.

No one, perhaps not even the Kurds themselves, knew who they really were, what they could achieve in the modern world, given what they had been through. We in the West knew them mainly from photos of their dead or from images of hundreds of thousands fleeing into the mountains or from television interviews with overwhelmed and not yet camera-ready Kurdish politicians.

Few Westerners, and only a tiny portion of Americans, could have guessed how much of these amazing people had been driven below the surface or how much of their skill and grace had been lost. Yet this was beginning to change. Remember that this was in the early 1990s. A no-fly zone had just begun to allow the Kurds the freedom to breathe easy. Saddam was held in check for the moment. The Turks were pressing but not invading from the north. There was a civil war troubling the land, but it was minor given what the Kurds had been through— the *Anfal* with its gassings and strafing and tortures. One Kurd described his people to me at this time as being like gophers tentatively popping their heads above ground after a heavy rain.

The significance of this emergence of the Kurds—in the world and even within themselves—is only understandable when we come to appreciate how powerful are the unique characteristics of the Kurds, how much their astonishing distinctives surged for release from deep within their individual and corporate souls.

Among my favorite illustrations of this centers upon a Columbia University archaeologist named Ralph Solecki. It was during the 1960s and Solecki was heading up a dig for Paleolithic human remains in the Shanidar Cave of central Kurdistan. To accomplish this tedious work, Solecki hired dozens of workers from the surrounding region—which meant, of course, Kurds. The work had just begun when Solecki noticed something strange was happening. The Kurds had begun attaching flowers to everything in sight. On their axes and picks. On the water trucks. On the walls of the caves. Even on themselves. Individual flowers, bouquets of flowers, and flowers tied into various shapes appeared everywhere throughout the otherwise colorless and aesthetically uninteresting site.

Solecki, who seems to have been a truly humorless soul at the time, spent large portions of his written reports complaining about the flowers and the Kurds. However, he also reported that his excavation had uncovered the remains of a man whom Solecki believed had lived 56,000 years before. This proved important, for Solecki's team had not only discovered the remains of this Paleolithic man, but they also discovered that this man—buried all those thousands of years before—was laid to rest on a palette of flowers—in fact, on a lush bed made from a great variety of flowers. Laboratory tests confirmed it.

So there the irritated archaeologist was, watching his flower-strewn Kurdish workers dig through the floor of a cave only to find that these Kurds were maintaining some of the oldest of human traditions and, perhaps unknowingly, expressing distinctly Kurdish passions that had survived in their people for centuries. Indeed, it was the Kurds who best represented the historic ways of mankind, not Solecki.

Even Solecki came to admit this. Apparently, the scholar also acquired a greater capacity for humor than seemed possible at first. He titled his 1971 excavation report, *Shanidar: The First Flower People*. This was Solecki's nod not only to the youth culture that pervaded the universities at the time but also to the Kurds Solecki knew and their brightly colored approach to life.[2]

I thought often about this surprising feature of the Kurdish soul—their passion for flowers and color—and was saddened at the thought of it being driven underground by wars and persecutions, by terrifying seasons of state-imposed famine and mass execution. The ugliness of much that the Kurds were forced to endure swallowed such things as flowers and color, leaving only a drab, muddy existence. It was the same with many of the wonderful, joyous traits of the Kurds. They had been buried in the ground during a frozen winter season. I tried to feel something of the Kurds' ache to return to who they truly were and perhaps their confusion when freedom came and their uniqueness began to reemerge.

This reclaiming of colors signaled the great thaw underway. It might seem insignificant until we understand how much it is at the heart of what it means to be Kurdish. Of course, color is a passion throughout the Middle East and in many cultures of the world. Still, it is hard to find a people more insanely devoted to great, dramatic splashes of color than the Kurds. One of their own chroniclers has written, "Riotous and gaudy colors, many, many of them, thrown together seemingly haphazardly, with absolutely no control or care to match them, is the trademark of the Kurdish taste. It makes a Kurd stand out in any crowd of conventionally dressed people, in the ancient times as now."[3]

This is no overstatement. Kurds love brilliant colors in every combination and on every surface possible. If they decide to pay tribute to a particularly old tree, they do it by attaching great swatches of colored cloth to the branches. When they buy a new appliance, one that might appear sleek and modern to western eyes, many Kurds feel the need to make sure that the device is "housebroken"—which means that they splash it with color to make it one with the rest of their home. This passion for color has deep roots in their history. One of their ancestral religions assigned a color to every day of the week and to each of its seven gods.

Many were the times I returned to the U.S. after weeks in Kurdistan carrying gifts from my Kurdish friends. Upon opening my suitcase and passing these gifts to my wife and children, we would notice the near luminescent color of every object. Our house was far from drab but these gifts were so bright they nearly made it seem so. The colors of Kurdish cloth and painting, of tea cozies and head scarves, were so dazzling that they seemed more akin to the children's toys in their brilliance than what they truly were—cherished gifts from adult friends.

Kurdish art captures this same passion for color. Kurdish painter Mansour Ahmed once said, "For me painting is a way of altercation and coping with a given situation. In association with colors I find my distant home, I find my own self."[4] This is a helpful depiction of the Kurdish soul. Colors shout and clash because they represent the turmoil of the heart, the loud, conflicting emotions of life. A blank surface is like a life unlived. Colors must baptize the new toaster or it has not been drawn into the storm-ridden, changeable life of the owner.

The most touching example of this is the manner in which Kurds usually bury their dead. They envision a day when brilliantly colored flowers will grow on graves, but until that day arrives, vibrant cloth, paper, bows, and even a child's pinwheel suffice. Deceased infants can look to non-Kurdish eyes as though they have been "gift-wrapped."[5]

This fascination for, even desperation for, color is part of a broader reality of the Kurds that I see as a symptom of their suffering. They seem to carry within them a universe of color, movement, story and joy that is almost entirely belied by their outer appearance. Of course, no people in the world show all they feel or think at the surface. The Kurds, however, are astonishingly concealed and it is surely a result of their hard lives and the constant, angry gaze of the tyrants who have tried to grind them from history.

I have already described the changeable face of my friend Asan. I found the same tendency on faces throughout Kurdistan. The experience repeated itself so often that it almost became a game to me. I would exit a vehicle and walk toward the door of a building. The armed guard at that door—for in those days there were always armed guards— would stare at me with a severe, almost angry look. I would keep walking. He would stand, no change in his face at all. When I got to the appropriate distance, I would raise my right hand just above my head, palm turned inward, and offer the Kurdish word for hello.

It is natural that a wave and a kind word would ease the tension an armed guard might feel at an approaching stranger. Since the guard was holding a machine gun, I—the approaching stranger—was happy to see the tension lift as well. What was even more beautiful to see, though, was the explosion of those wizened, stark faces into brilliant, cheerful, unrestrained smiles. It was as though all that was required for happiness to surface was for a friend to make himself known. I was absolutely fascinated by this and loved each time a seemingly ancient, wary visage gave way to an almost childlike delight. I had to believe that this glaring manner came from the years when survival depended upon betraying nothing publicly.

Time and again the Kurds shocked me with some hidden, seemingly ancient passion surfacing like a great subterranean sea suddenly exploding upward, gushing through the dry, hardened earth. Among the most memorable of these experiences had to do with the Kurds and dancing. On more than one occasion, I would be sitting among a group of Kurds who seemed intent upon their duties and the pressing issues of the moment when dancing would break out like joyous play among children. It was as though the true Kurdish soul would suddenly erupt in a grand explosion of cheering and movement. It was beautiful and mystifying all at the same time.

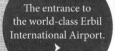

The entrance to the world-class Erbil International Airport.

CREDIT: © Jeffrey Beall

One of the many palaces Saddam Hussein built became a U.S. military headquarters at Camp Victory in Iraq.

The Citadel of Erbil is likely the oldest continuously inhabited town in the world—8,000 years.

CREDIT: © Ask Gudmundsen

The main square in Erbil, near the Citadel's South Gate and between the two main bazaars.

CREDIT: © Ask Gudmundsen

The new, state-of-the-art campus at The American University of Iraq, Sulimaniya.

CREDIT: © Diyar se

The author in the foothills of the mountains of Kurdistan.

The author prepares to leave Kurdistan and its snow-capped mountains by boat in 1997.

The author sits on the throne from which Saddam Hussein intended to rule the Middle East.

The author with a bodyguard in 1998.

Kurdish Peshmerga cook bread over an open fire in the mountains of Kurdistan.

These remains found in a mass grave confirm that Iraqi soldiers shot Kurdish infants and sometimes buried them alive.

NORTH

This computer-generated image shows the number and positions of bodies uncovered in one of the many mass graves hastily dug by Iraqi troops.

NINAWA0009

Distribution of Bodies
Date of Recovery

1   0   1 Meters

25 Sep
27 Sep
28 Sep
30 Sep
01 Oct
02 Oct
03 Oct
Saponified Remains
Trench Floor

Excavations

SAChomko
08Apr05

A father desperately tried to protect his infant son during the gassings at Halabjah. Both father and son were killed.
➤

The gassings of Halabjah begin—March 16, 1988.

A Kurdish girl weeps for the dead of Kurdistan.
➤

A mother and a father weep over their dead loved ones.

Bodies of Kurds gassed at Halabjah are loaded onto trucks for burial.

Caskets of the dead are readied for a funeral after a huge mass grave was discovered in Kurdistan.

حکومەتی هەرێمی کوردستان
وەزارەتی کاروباری شەهیدان و ئەنفالکراوەکان

MINISTRY OF MARTYRS & ANFAL AFFAIRS

The Archives of a peoples' suffering: The Ministry of Martyrs and Anfal Affairs in Erbil.
◄

The author meeting with the senior mullah of Kurdistan, Abdullah Saeed Aloisi.
▶

◄
General Kurdwan Sheik Mahmoud Al Naqshbandy stands at the Halabjah Memorial in Kurdistan.

Jalal Talabani, the sixth president of Iraq, known as "Uncle Jalal" among Kurds.
▼

Kurdistan Regional Government President Massoud Barzani with President George W. Bush.

CREDIT: © White House photo by Eric Draper

CREDIT: U.S. Department of Defense / Helene C. Stikkel

Pastor Yousif Matti al Qas, founder of the Classical School of the Medes.

Mullah Mustafa Barzani, the "George Washington" of the Kurds.

The author with dissident Kurds in Turkey.

Kurdish men in traditional clothing. These men were killed at Halabjah.

The city of Sulimaniya with the Grand Millennium Hotel in the center.

Erbil city center at night.

The Erbil Rotana Hotel.

The Sofi Mall in Erbil.

There was a particular afternoon when I happened to be among a fairly large number of Kurdish men, all of whom were well armed and all of whom seemed thoroughly consumed with tending to the military concerns of the moment. While I watched these men scurry about their work, there was suddenly a whoop of delight from some younger Kurds standing at the side of an old building. When I looked in the direction of the sound, I saw three or four men cheering as another of them began gyrating his shoulders in rapid, almost sensuous ways. There was sheer delight on each face. I quickly realized that a dance was revving up and that the young man moving with stunning speed was known for his skills. Other men began hurrying over to the commotion and while I could not understand what they were saying to each other, it had the joy and urgency of something like, "Hey, Bizad is going to dance! Let's hurry and see!"

Within moments, other young men moved to the side of the dancer, joined hands and began imitating his astonishing gyrations. Dozens formed a great line, all moving in unison, while the rest clapped and laughed with delight. Remember that just five minutes before this had been an armed camp of men seemingly preparing for battle. Now, it was the scene of men celebrating in unreserved joy. Celebrating what, I wondered. I never found out. The celebrating itself seemed to be the point.

I was standing at the side of this commotion when two men, fierce and foreboding just moments before, approached me with broad smiles and said, "Come, Mr. Stephen, you must join us." I should tell you that I am six feet, four inches tall and at the time hovered around 250 pounds. This means I was nearly twice the size of any Kurd there. It made no difference at all to my hosts.

Within seconds, I was urged into the line of dancing men and expected to imitate their movements. It was never going to happen. I could come close to repeating the gentle rhythms of the entire dancing line. Yet when one of the men stepped out from the line and began his unique, sinewy dance, I quickly realized I would need to watch a video replay over and over again to even understand what he was doing, much less imitate it.

Realizing my plight, the men laughed and clapped more uproariously. It had all come in a moment and after a half an hour or so it dissipated just as quickly with backslaps and smiles. I had never seen anything like it. It was an eruption of joy and dance I would never have associated with military men and certainly never have expected of guerrilla fighters in a war zone. It was another demonstration that the Kurds do life their own way, that they remake their world into a distinctly Kurdish form.

I had dozens of experiences like this. The Kurdish love of laughter and humor provided more than a few of them.

Again, they surprised. Again, it seemed they had been holding in check the most wonderful of their gifts, laughter among them. All people love to laugh, of course, and most love a good joke. The Kurds, once they allow themselves, can laugh as though happy, unrestrained laughter is part of their destiny.

Once I was in an SUV with two bodyguards and another Kurdish friend as we drove from Sulimaniya to Duhok. The three were alert and intensely focused throughout most of the trip. It was a dangerous time. I became bored with this, though, and began asking questions. With their answers came a lighter mood and then one of them told a joke.

It seems there was a tribe known for its rustic, gullible people. A man from that tribe bought his first cell phone and was driving along one day when the thing rang. It was his daughter. The stunned man couldn't believe it. "How did you know where I am?!" he asked.

Now, this joke would warrant no more than a courtesy laugh most anywhere else in the world. Yet my three Kurdish friends were so undone by it that they nearly got me killed. We were driving on mountain roads at the time. The driver, a steely Peshmerga, bellowed so uncontrollably that he allowed the vehicle to weave from side to side. Finally, I insisted he pull to the edge of the road until he was done. There we sat for what felt like fifteen minutes while my three nitwit Kurdish friends behaved as though this was the joke that made all other jokes unnecessary.

When they finally recovered themselves, we moved on. But it just wouldn't end. For the remainder of the drive, one of them would erupt again about every twenty minutes. It reminded me of high school. I would have put the whole episode down to exhaustion, except that I found this happening time and time again throughout Kurdistan.

These examples—of the Kurds and the Jews, of flowers and color, of laughter and dance—capture the nature of the Kurdish difference and how they make the features of their world their own. These are important for their own sake, but they also serve to point to what may be the most valuable distinctive of the Kurds to the wider world today: the way they have also remade Islam in their own image.

Islam has troubled the New World since long before the idea of a nation called the United States arose. Alien as Islam was to those who first came to these shores, the fate of the Muslim world weighed heavily upon their minds.

Of all that motivated Christopher Columbus to sail to the New World, among them was his hope of gaining wealth with which to retake the Holy Land from Muslim armies. As he wrote to the sovereigns who commissioned him:

I hope to God that when I come back here from Castile ... that I will find ... gold ... in such quantities that within three years the Sovereign will prepare for and undertake the reconquest of the Holy Land. I have already petitioned Your Highnesses to see that all the profits of this, my enterprise, should be spent on the conquest of Jerusalem, and Your Highnesses smiled and said that the idea pleased them, and that even without the expedition they had the inclination to do it.[6]

Though later generations may have laid aside the idea of reclaiming the Holy Land, most thought no differently about Islam itself. In 1773, during the great religious movement that swept through the American colonies just before the Revolution, eminent theologian Jonathan Edwards described in his *History of Redemption* what his generation believed about the eventual fall of Mahometanism.

Satan's Mahometan kingdom shall be utterly overthrown. And then—though Mahometanism has been so vastly propagated in the world, and is upheld by such a great empire—this smoke, which has ascended out of the bottomless pit, shall be utterly scattered before the light of that glorious day, and the Mahometan empire shall fall at the sound of the great trumpet which shall then be blown.[7]

Prophecies such as this were widely circulated during the Great Awakening and the Revolution that came afterward. It may have come as little surprise to some early Americans, then, that the first war fought by the new United States was against Muslim forces. We remember this Tripolitan War each time the United States Marines tell us in song that they were fashioned first "on the shores of Tripoli."

Animosities toward Islam dimmed but did not disappear through the next century and a half of American history. They were revived when a plague of Islamic terrorism beset the nation and led eventually to the September 11, 2001, attacks on New York's World Trade Center and the Pentagon in Washington DC. Wars followed and then attempts at refashioning Islamic nations into Islamic democracies. None of it endeared the U.S. to the Muslim world. Not even the efforts of a conciliatory and Muslim-friendly Obama presidency could halt the downward spiral.

It has not helped that Americans know little about the religions of the world, Islam in particular. At the time of the 2012 presidential election, more than 20 percent of Americans believed that Barack Obama was a Muslim, despite the fact that he claimed to be a Christian, attended Christian worship services regularly, and had only practiced Islam briefly during a few childhood years spent in Indonesia.

This misperception was born of a broader ignorance. Surveys have repeatedly shown that more than half of all Americans know little to nothing of the Islamic faith. After the infamous 9/11 attacks, Sikhs were beaten on the streets of New York by men who could not distinguish the followers of Guru Nanak from the followers of Muhammad. Synagogues were damaged by similarly minded men who could not distinguish between Muslims and Jews. It was not an uncommon failing at the time and may not be all that uncommon now.

We are a people distanced from Islam by our history, distanced by our offense with Islamic terrorism and distanced by our ignorance of who Muslims are and what they believe. We are also distanced by features of Islam itself. Because it is forbidden by Islamic law to translate the original manuscripts of the Koran for fear of corruptions and theological errors, there is no official or at least definitive English translation. Even the most basic terms of the faith are left to multiple-choice. Is it *Qu'ran, Quran, Ku'ron,* or *Koran*? Is it *Muslims, Moslems,* or *Muhammadans*? Is it *Mohammed, Mohamet, Mohomet,* or *Muhammad*? Americans, having little patience for theological distinctions to begin with, are not likely to wade through these or far more important mysteries.

Yet the United States will be contending with the influence of Islam for decades to come. By 2030, Muslims will represent more than a quarter of the world's population. It will not be possible, even if Islamic terrorism should completely disappear, for Americans to function on the global stage without understanding Islam and nurturing fruitful relationships with Islamic partners.

This trend will make the Kurds and their approach to Islam of great value to the United States. Though three-fifths of all Kurds are Muslim, they have done to religion what they do to nearly everything that comes into their hands: they have remade it in their own more tolerant, uniquely Kurdish image.

At a time when Muslim fundamentalists seem to be in the ascent throughout the Middle East—a time when violence reigns, revolutions produce little but pain, and Christians are systematically exterminated—the Kurds have nurtured a gentler, more inclusive, more workable brand of Islam that ought to be a model for the world.

I know this because the Chief Mullah of all Kurdistan told me it was true. His name is Abdullah Saeed Aloisi. I spent some of the more fascinating hours of my life in conversation with this man. Nothing could have prepared me for his sophistication, broad-mindedness, and fearlessness.

He was a younger man than I expected, particularly given his influential position. He was well-read, knowledgeable about the Western world, and had an easy manner that I found endearing. Though he was intensely serious, as mullahs tend to be, he was quick to smile and eager without being pushy that I understand him. More specifically, he wanted me to understand how the Kurdish version of Islam is not that of the wider Muslim world.

In the first five minutes of our conversation, the Mullah told me that Arab Islamic organizations were working to undermine the Kurds and he had taken a stand against it. He accepted the fact that traditional Islam was sometimes more a process of "Arabization" than of teaching men to obey Allah and that he was working to make sure this did not happen in Kurdistan.[8] Already there was a Kurdish language Koran. He spoke of it proudly. He intended to translate commentaries into Kurdish, assure that some ceremonies and documents could be done in Kurdish, and that there would be schools for clerics in which Kurdish languages were spoken. There were ceremonies that should only be done in Arabic, the holy Muslim language. He accepted this. He believed in it. But he would not allow Islam in Kurdistan to become an excuse for Arab domination.

I should mention again that I was talking to Abdullah Saeed Aloisi, the Chief Mullah of Kurdistan. I say this because I had to remind myself of this fact often as I listened to the man. It was difficult to hide my shock. These are views rarely discussed in the Islamic world, much less boldly broached with a visiting American Christian.

Mullah Aloisi wasn't finished. He admitted he was being accused of "some things" by clerics in Turkey and Iran.

"We do have disagreements. These can become personal disagreements." Some of these critics "do not want to let our message pass. But we care about our people. And this is my country."

I wanted to stand and cheer the man. It was moving. This is when I joked that I had felt safe in his country until this meeting and now he, the senior Muslim in the country, was about to put me, the visiting American, in peril with Muslims. He laughed loudly at this and then said, in essence, "we are both in the hands of Allah."

He returned to his subject: the uniqueness of Kurdish Islam and how it set him in tension with clerics of other nations. He said that the world should remember that Saddam used Islam against the Kurds and that this was sure to shape Kurdish Islam for many years.

It was a point I had intended to bring up with him, but he beat me to it. One of the worst cruelties visited upon the Kurds was the *Al-Anfal* campaign. It was vicious in its tactics—artillery, gas, air raids, rape, torture and most of it against unarmed civilians—but it was also devastating to the Kurds' religion because the very name was taken from the Holy Koran.

I knew that *Al-Anfal* meant "The Spoils," as in "spoils of war," and that it was the name of a chapter in the Koran. The Mullah explained that this eighth *sura* or chapter of the Koran described a battle that occurred in 624 AD, a battle in which some three hundred Muslims defeated nine hundred nonbelievers. It was Saddam Hussein's favorite chapter of the Koran because it encouraged killing of non-believers and the taking of "booty" from defeated enemies. Saddam named his campaign of genocide against Kurds after this chapter of the Koran.

"When your faith has been used against you to murder your people—1,200 Kurdish villages were destroyed, perhaps 180,000 Kurds dead—you will not think of your faith the same way again. You may believe, but you will not trust the faithful in the same way. Kurds will have their religion, but it will be a religion in Kurdistan, not just the religion of Arab lands."

While the English translation came, the Mullah looked at me firmly, almost as though to say, "Yes, I said that." Once I understood, I looked back at him and shook my head with eyebrows raised as though to say, "Wow. What an amazing thing you've said." He smiled and looked down. It was the only time we communicated directly—meaning without our interpreters— other than shaking hands and it was a deeply meaningful moment. I've spoken to many Muslim clerics in my life. None like this man.

I asked him, finally, about his vision or dream for Kurdistan. He said, "I cannot even count my dreams for Kurdistan as a religious man. We have a dream to recognize our identity as a country and raise the flag of Kurdistan at the United Nations. Some will talk about it. Others try to hide it. But it is our dream."

The Mullah clearly wanted his religion, but he wanted it Kurdish style. This came as no surprise. I had learned by then that Kurds make their world Kurdish and this included religion. I was not prepared for his plainspokenness or the intensity of his love for Kurdistan. I was not prepared for the price he was willing to pay.

The Kurdish experience and Kurdish leaders of this caliber have made Kurdish Islam a religion far removed from what is common in the world. It is evident throughout their land.

It begins with the tempering that comes from Kurds being of a variety of religions: Muslim, Christian, Jew, Yezidi, Sufi, and Baha'i with a smattering of others. These faiths are not just tolerated. They are part of the Kurdish whole.

There is a measured approach also to civil rights. Women still have a long road to travel towards their full rights, but there are female Supreme Court and lower court judges in Kurdistan, female heads of government departments, and successful female entrepreneurs. Women are as likely to be without the traditional veil on the streets as they are to wear it.

There is a Christian department within the regional government. It shares a hallway with the Yezidi department and the Muslim department. There is also a minster of religion. It sounds odd in English, but it is true.

The public schools favor no single religion but teach them all. One of the largest and most successful schools in Kurdistan is quietly Christian and it is an open secret. Most of the students who attend come from Muslim families.

Then there is this amazing mullah, who would probably be shot or exiled if he lived in a neighboring Muslim country. Not in Kurdistan. Would to God that every Muslim cleric on earth should be like Abdullah Saeed Aloisi.

The conclusion is that Kurdish Islam is one of the most moderate versions of that faith in the world. It is so because the Kurds themselves, despite their history as a warring people, are among the gentlest and most poetic people in the world. This is what we are learning in the Great Thaw of the Kurdish people and it gives promise of what the Kurds, their faith, and their part of the world may well become. We should hope that Kurdistan might become a model for all of these Kurdish virtues.

Yet it is these very Kurdish distinctives that so enrage the Kurds' enemies. They will not conform. They insist on being Kurdish. Their heritage, their mountains, their gentle spirit, their treatment by fellow Muslims and their unique history set them apart. Those who demand conformity despise them for it, none so viciously as Saddam Hussein. He dreamt of an Arab world, of a resurgent and global Babylonian Empire. The Kurds refused. They were not Arabs, they wished no empire and they would not do a tyrant's bidding. So, Saddam slaughtered them by the hundreds of thousands. There is no understanding the Kurdish rise of our day, until we first understand the evil that sought to crush the Kurds from their land and from the pages of history itself.

CHAPTER 6

THE "CRASHER"

*"Sooner or later the Saddam Hussein regime will fall,
either of its own weight or from the physical and mental
collapse of its leader or from endogenous or exogenous
pressure. On that day one will want to be able to look the
Iraqi and Kurdish people in the eye and say that we thought
seriously about their interest and appreciated that, because
of previous interventions that were actually in Saddam's favor,
we owed them a debt. It's this dimension that seems to me
lacking in the current antiwar critique."*

—Christopher Hitchens[1]

There was a moment in my life when I felt the pure,
terrifying evil of Saddam Hussein. I never met him
personally, of course, nor was I ever under much threat
from his tactics against the Kurds. Yet there was one
searing moment when I had as mystical an experience as

I have ever had. It was an experience of the demonic force that empowered Saddam Hussein.

It was early in 2005, a year after Saddam's capture and two years before his execution. I was embedded with U.S. troops at Camp Victory in Iraq. I was there to explore the influence religion was having upon the young generation at war. As always, I intended to write a book about the subject. Something interesting was happening among our troops. Reporters described it as a quiet revival in the ranks. *The New York Times* and *The Washington Post* reported occurrences like Marines being baptized in the sands of Iraq and soldiers listening to worship music while they drove their Humvees into battle. I wanted to find out firsthand what was happening. Gratefully, the Pentagon gave me permission to do it.

That's how I came to be in one of Saddam's palaces. It was an enormous building of concrete and stone wrapped by a huge pond—a moat, really—that sat on the grounds of Camp Victory, just outside of Baghdad. Nearly every day I was in-country, I walked from tents, trailers, and sandbagged embankments past the moat through three-story entrances that led inside to a massive atrium. The scene was both absurd and exhilarating. The ostentation the dictator demanded for himself was sickening. I was grateful that much of it had been stripped away. Yet I was deeply moved by the sight of fully armed American troops rushing back and forth, doing the business they were sent to do, and in a building Saddam intended as a palace of perversion, a threatening symbol of one man's complete domination of a nation.

I had been to the building several times during my visit before I walked through the atrium with Colonel Gene Fowler. He was the senior chaplain at Camp Victory and his permission had made my trip possible. As we made our way to a meeting upstairs, Col. Fowler suddenly turned to me and asked if I had noticed a huge chair that sat near the atrium wall. I hadn't.

I was stunned. Then I was delighted. The thing sat amidst other unused furniture, no one paying attention to it in the busyness of the day. It struck me that this is how all thrones of all dictators should be treated: ignored in the storage rooms of liberators.

Col. Fowler asked me if I wanted to sit on it. I hesitated. I did not want to honor the vile thing by showing too much fascination. Then I realized I was—fascinated. What kind of throne does an evil man fashion for himself? I should know, I told myself, if I was going to understand this war.

As I seated myself, I was aware of its gaudy enormity. Four men my size could have fit on it. It was the kind of seat a man builds envisioning enemies kissing his hand and officials groveling. It was designed for a man who was compensating.

I was about to joke about this to Col. Fowler when I felt a sort of inner flash. Nothing changed about the throne or me, but I suddenly felt the evil of the thing. I had the sensation that I was sitting on a throne built of skulls. It was as though all the lives sacrificed in Saddam's ravenous pursuit of power were imprisoned inside that throne, each one represented by a skull.

The sensation lasted only a few seconds. I was grateful for it. I had been touring an Iraq that seemed a monument to Saddam's malevolence, but somehow I had not felt it as I knew I should. I understood what had happened but had not touched the horror of it. A few seconds on that evil throne allowed me to feel all the oppression and darkness I ever hope to.

I certainly recognize that this was a subjective experience. I don't expect those who hear of it to understand it or even to believe that it happened. Here is what I do know: I felt for a few seconds—Physically? Emotionally? Spiritually? I don't know—what I perceived to be a dictator's murderous wickedness. The experience has never left me. Yet hundreds of thousands of human beings, most of them Kurds, lived for years under that darkness and then were extinguished by it. The nearly indescribable horror of this is something we should force ourselves to understand, for we will never comprehend the enormity of the miracle happening among the Kurds in our time unless we face their sufferings truthfully and allow ourselves to carry a bit of their grief in our souls.

He was a good man. His name was Dr. Raji al-Tikriti. He was brilliant. Born in Tikrit, Iraq, as his name suggests, he so distinguished himself academically as a young man that he was sent to England to earn a degree in neurosurgery He became a highly skilled physician and ultimately one of Iraq's leading experts on spinal injuries. He advised the Iraqi Air Force on the design of ejection seats in fighters and urged other innovations that saved lives and prevented crippling accidents. In time, he became the commanding general of the Iraqi Army medical corps. He was held in great esteem. Many a man in uniform owed his health, if not his life, to Dr. al-Tikriti.

Yet he was, as most brilliant men are, opinionated. Sitting among a group of fellow doctors one day, he expressed the kind of opinion that would have gone without notice in most of the world. "Who is Saddam Hussein?" he asked. "He grew up in the streets of Tikrit. He's uneducated, and he only became president because he'll stop at nothing."

Had he spoken these words in New York or Moscow or Johannesburg, little would have come of it. Foolishly, he had dared to speak these words in Iraq. Saddam Hussein's Iraq. The Baath party was everywhere—sensitive to disloyalty and vengeful of dissident opinions. Like those of Dr. Raji al-Tikriti.

Several weeks later, the phone rang at the Iraqi embassy in Amman, Jordan. Ambassador Nouri Al-Weis was summoned to the phone and was stunned to hear the voice of President Saddam Hussein calling from Baghdad.

"I understand that Dr. Raji al-Tikriti is in Jordan," the president said coolly. "Have you seen him?"

The ambassador was surprised. "Why, yes, sir. He's sitting here with me now."

Again, the calm, controlled voice from Baghdad. "Nouri, whatever you do, don't let him leave. I want you to give him your car and send him to me as soon as possible. I need to see him urgently." The ambassador did as he was told and Raji al-Tikriti was quickly returned to Baghdad, everyone assuming that the president was ill and needed care from one of the nation's best doctors.

When he arrived at the presidential palace, Dr. Raji was taken to a room in the basement. There, sixty large, muscular guards took him in hand. There was a pause. Several of the guards looked to one side of the room where a figure sat calmly, his legs crossed as he slowly lit a large Havana cigar. It was Saddam Hussein. He did not speak at first. He seemed to be enjoying the moment. Then, coldly, he said, "Okay, do it."

At this signal, one of the powerfully built guards struck Dr. Raji to the ground. The rest began to stomp the man with their heavy, hobnail boots. As though in a frenzy, the guards kicked viciously, at times jumping high into the air to land on their victim.

This continued until there was little left but human jelly spread upon the basement floor. Saddam registered no emotion. He gave another signal. Guards dutifully opened a kennel door and loosed a pack of large, starving dogs. The animals ran straight to the remains of Dr. Raji and began devouring him. In moments, there was nothing left. Saddam looked on stoically as the snarling animals licked the last smudges of blood from the concrete floor.

It was a ghastly scene, typical of Saddam Hussein's sadism. There were thousands of episodes like it: ritual rapes, the slow dismemberment of chained prisoners, the crude decapitating of party enemies, the smashing of infants against bedroom walls while mothers looked on. And there were the gassings, as we shall see. Hundreds of thousands of lives were ended in blood and blasphemous torture. It is difficult to exaggerate the immensity of it all.

There is no explaining the monsters of history. There are only the facts and the labor of generations to comprehend the evil. This is the legacy of Saddam Hussein.

He grew up—like Dr. Raji al-Tikriti—in the hardscrabble town of Tikrit. So rugged is the land and so hardened the people of that region, that some of the fiercest of warriors in history have arisen from there, men renowned for battle since before the Ottoman Empire.

The name *Saddam* is best translated "the crasher." It is an odd name for a child but then Saddam's childhood circumstances were odder still. His father died while the future dictator was still in the womb. His mother eventually abandoned him. He was raised as an orphan. He was big, rough mannered, and mentally slow. As a result, he started school much later than other children. His size allowed him to overcome the shame by bullying. His uncle, Khairullah Tilfah, was as near to a parent as Saddam ever had but he was a cruel, treacherous man. The boy learned well.

He became a street tough, a thug. He led a gang of boys like him and gained a reputation for ruthlessness. He thought nothing of torture and murder. He never finished school. There were entire subjects in which he did not possess the basic knowledge of a child and men gave their lives in later years for speaking of it. He was, simply put, a gangster and this is what brought him to the attention of the Baath Socialist Party. Ever grasping power through intimidation and turmoil, the Baathists made Saddam an enforcer when he was still in his teens and then, after he proved himself, offered him a special assignment. He was assigned the task of assassinating Abdel Karim Qassem, the president of Iraq. He was twenty-two years old.

On the appointed day, Saddam and his gang opened fire on the president's vehicles as they moved along Al Rashind Street in downtown Baghdad. Undisciplined and over-excited, the inexperienced assassins fired hundreds of erratic shots. When they were done, Saddam ran to the president's car and sprayed it with machine gun fire. President Qassem was wounded but not killed. His bodyguards repelled the attack and secured medical care so swiftly that they saved Qassem's life. He lived to hold power for another three years.

Saddam was wounded in the attack, though, and limped off into the teeming city in search of help. Running out of time and finding no doctor willing to take the risk, he used his knife to dig the bullet out of his own flesh. When he was well enough to travel, he crossed into Syria and remained in hiding there for four years.

He returned to Iraq in 1963 when President Qassem was ousted by the Baathists in what is remembered as the Ramadan Revolution, led by Abdel-Salaam Aref and Ahmed Hassan al-Bakr. Saddam was particularly close to al-Bakr, who was both the general secretary of the party and a relative. The two men were from Tikrit and were of the same tribe and the same family.

The new Baathist government was plagued with dissension and fractured quickly. Saddam was imprisoned in 1964, escaped in 1967, and began to distinguish himself as an organizer and party leader. When the Baathists initiated a second coup in 1968, Saddam became the new president's deputy.

He proved as ruthless to his allies as he was to his enemies. Just two weeks after the coup, Saddam walked into the prime minister's office with a gun and told the man, "Either I will kill you now or you're finished. Choose the place you want to travel to." The terrified prime minster protested: "Saddam, why are you doing this?" The thug from Tikrit said simply, "Don't talk much. It's over." The deposed official was forced into exile in London where not long afterwards he was gunned down in the street by his own military attaché—just as Saddam had ordered. Ahmed Hassan al-Bakr became the president, prime minister, and minister of defense of Iraq. Saddam Hussein served as his deputy.

No one who knew Saddam believed he would content himself with a secondary role. He used his time wisely, though. He carefully cultivated a reputation as the man who could get things done. He let al-Bakr play the figurehead while he accumulated true power, the kind that comes from graft, bribes, intimidation, and buying the support of the powerful. As he grasped for control and influence, he also began creating his own myth. This led to the day he walked into the president's office and insisted upon having military rank in order to run the affairs of government. Intimidated officials quickly made Saddam a four-star general though he had never completed a single hour of military training. Legitimate military officers were soon shocked to see Saddam wearing the ribbon worn only by Staff College graduates. "The Crasher" had never finished high school.

Still ravenous for power, Saddam persuaded al-Bakr that the two should share authority, that the deputy should be equal to the president. This would allow documents to be signed for the busy senior man and make his work easier. Al-Bakr knew better than to deny Saddam any privilege. Iraqis began speaking of a "two for one" presidency. Protocol required that a congratulatory remark extended to the president should not be extended to al-Bakr alone but rather to the "president and his distinguished deputy." Saddam had written the rules.

This arrangement lasted from 1968 until 1979 when Saddam grew weary of the pretense. He told al-Bakr, as he had told an earlier prime minister, to leave office or die. So it was that in 1979 an uneducated, sadistic, egomaniacal street thug became the president and prime minister of Iraq. "The Crasher" had prevailed.

Saddam installed himself in his new role in a manner that signaled the horrors to come. To understand the hideous forces at work in the new regime, it is worth quoting journalist Christopher Hitchens, who was able to obtain a video showing how Saddam confirmed himself in power during a plenary session of the Ba'ath party central committee with around hundred men in attendance.

> Into the room is dragged an obviously broken man, who begins to emit a robotic confession of treason and subversion ... As the extorted confession unfolds, names begin to be named. Once a fellow-conspirator is identified, guards come to his seat and haul him from the room. The reclining Saddam, meanwhile, lights a large cigar and contentedly scans his dossiers. The sickness of fear in the room is such that men begin to crack up and weep, rising to their feet to shout hysterical praise, even love, for the leader ... When it is over, about half the committee members are left ... (In an accompanying sequel, which I have not seen, they were apparently required to go into the yard outside and shoot the other half, thus sealing the pact with Saddam.)[2]

Thus began the domination of Iraq. Saddam treated the country like his personal fiefdom, draining its wealth for his every whim, murdering those who opposed him. He first impoverished the Iraqi people, then he endangered them. He grew the military to 6,400 tanks, 40 regiments of artillery, and over 1,000 combat aircraft. From the Baathists he had learned how to confiscate the profits of the oil fields for state purposes. He now did the same for himself. Palaces sprang up around the country, sixty-eight in all. Cars and presidential helicopters and ever more fanciful titles and uniforms were added to his possessions. No comfort, no woman, no symbol of prestige, and no excess were denied him.

He ordered expedited development of chemical weapons and made it clear to the world he intended to build Iraq into a nuclear super power. He became obsessed with missiles, particularly the now infamous SCUD missile, designed by the Soviets and enhanced time and again by Iraqi technicians under strict orders from Saddam. Once he possessed SCUDs with double fuel tanks—which gave them a range of five hundred miles—he made it clear he intended to remake the entire Middle East in his own image.

He was a man possessed yet not by ego alone. What an increasingly terrified world either failed to understand or failed to take seriously was that Saddam had begun to see himself as the embodiment of a resurrected Babylonian Empire. An Iraqi Ministry of Information and Culture brochure made this startlingly clear.

Saddam Hussein has emerged from Mesopotamia as did Hammurabi, as did Merodach-baladan, and as did Nebuchadnezzar. He has emerged to shake the centuries-old dust off Babylon's face. History must start with us so that Babylon can remain mankind's compass throughout the ages. Spirit arise.[3]

Yet men addicted to power are usually insecure men who are ever paranoid of conspiracies against them. Saddam was no different. The complicated ethnic and religious patchwork that is Iraq did nothing to ease his fears. He was particularly concerned about the Shi'ites who populated the southern regions. Rumors of plans for a coup constantly swirled about the Shi'ites and in time, Saddam began to believe them. On April 8, 1980, in an astonishingly arrogant and foolish act, he ordered the assassination of the Grand Ayatollah Muhammad Baqir al-Sadr and his sister, Amina, the most visible and beloved Shi'ite leaders in Iraq.

The murders were intended as warnings to Iraqi Shi'ites, but they were also a sign of Saddam's belligerence toward neighboring Iran, a largely Shi'ite nation. Only the year before, the Shah of Iran, Muhammad Reza Pahlavi, had been deposed and the radical Shi'ite cleric Ayatollah Ruhollah Khomeini had assumed control of the country. Saddam feared that a Shi'ite revolution in Iran might spread to his own country. He also yearned to occupy land and waterways long claimed by Iran. Always, he dreamt of a modern Babylonian Empire ruling the Middle East.

From this fear and paranoia came the Iran-Iraq War. It was one of the most senseless wars of history. It proved nothing. It gained nothing for the combatants. It lasted eight carnage-filled years and left more than a million dead or wounded. Iran lost half a million souls. Iraq lost nearly three hundred thousand. Arms dealers in Europe and the United States sold weapons to both sides, guaranteeing a long and bloody conflict. The Iran-Iraq War was an atrocity from every perspective.

We should mark this moment in our story. It is 1988, a year no Kurd will forget. Indeed, Kurds will likely forget little of what was befalling them while the attention of the world was turned to the Iran-Iraq War, the Iranian Revolution, and the global impact of leaders like Ronald Reagan, Pope John Paul II, and Margaret Thatcher.

We should also mark 1988 because by then all that needed to be known of Saddam Hussein had been revealed. The nations knew who he was and what he would do. He had proven himself the vile "Crasher" to all who were willing to see, to all who possessed the moral clarity to understand what he had become.

He learned nothing from the bloodletting of the Iran-Iraq War. His vision of Babylonian rule was undimmed. Instead, in August of 1990, Saddam ordered the bombing of Kuwait City citing disputes over oil and boundaries. An invasion by the Iraqi army followed. After weeks of pillage and rumors of rape and murder, a U.S.-led coalition intervened and drove Iraqi forces out of Kuwait. Once coalition forces engaged on the ground, the war ended within one hundred hours. An Iraqi general boasted on international television that Iraq had launched "the mother of all battles." A U.S. general enjoyed countering that the war had quickly become "the mother of all retreats."

It was a humiliating defeat and should have resulted in the removal of Saddam from power. Instead, U.S. and European leaders decided to leave the tyrant in place to serve their purposes. It was a foolish move. Saddam convinced his nation that the thorough defeat of his troops was actually a victory—*Wasn't Iraq still standing after three powerful nations attacked it? Wasn't the president still in power? Wasn't the general who signed the treaty of surrender allowed to keep his pistol?*—and the following twelve years mirrored all that had come before. Saddam murdered the Marsh Arabs. He murdered Kurds. He murdered Shi'ites. He starved and brutalized the Iraqi people. He funded terrorism outside of Iraq. An Iraqi general estimated that nearly three hundred thousand people died under Saddam's oppressive regime during this time.

He was emboldened by what appeared to be American weakness. President George H. W. Bush had grown ineffective by the end of his term, Saddam believed. The

Clinton administration's policy of appeasement urged Saddam to even louder boasting, much to the Arab world's delight. When the U.S. did finally act against some provocation, it executed an air strike in Sudan that hit no designated target, but did extensive damage to an aspirin factory. The military intelligence behind the mission proved flawed, as did, it seemed, the whole of the United States. Saddam taunted that Americans were weak, their presidents were cowards, and it was time for the Arab world take their stand against "the Great Satan."

His bluster became his undoing. The beginning of the end came with the terrorist attacks on New York and Washington, DC, on September 11, 2001. Within months, President George W. Bush declared Iraq, Iran, and North Korea an "Axis of Evil." On March 19, 2003, a U.S.-led coalition swept into Iraq, exactly as Saddam had dared it to do. Twenty-one days later, a forty-foot-tall statue of Saddam in Baghdad's Fardus Square toppled to the ground. It was the symbol of the greater fact: Saddam had fallen. Children danced on the statue in joy. Old men beat it with their fists and then broke into uncontrollable weeping. Others stood near, their hands raised in thanksgiving to God.

Nine months after the fall of Baghdad, the man who had tortured Iraq for more than two decades was found hiding in a dank, smelly hole in the ground near his hometown of Tikrit. It was December 13, 2003. Iraqis were shocked at Saddam's appearance and his pitiful rants. Some had believed the madman's claim that he was invincible. Three years after, he was hanged for his crimes. Those present shouted the names of the dead as the dictator choked out his last breaths.

Our minds were not made to contemplate evil at great length. We inevitably protect ourselves by distorting and tempering. The mere process of trying to understand becomes a process of taming, of compacting. It is an attempt at intellectual anesthesia lest we be overwhelmed and brought to too much grief.

Still, we must find courage to face in peace and comfort what others have endured at the knife-edge of history. We dishonor those who suffer by retreating from their sickening truth and we shame ourselves in the process. An unswerving gaze upon history's atrocities is the best guarantee that those atrocities will not be repeated.

We must not rush past Saddam Hussein's deeds using easy terms like dictator or tyrant or madman. We cannot permit ourselves to sanitize. The specifics should live vitally in our minds and not be allowed to fade.

Saddam Hussein thought nothing of having his enemies partially amputated before giving them medical attention just so he could order his doctors to amputate again and again. He ordered the rape of women, the torture of children while their little bodies were chained to stone walls, the gassing of defenseless peasants, the machine gunning of old women, the assassination of distrusted officials, and the punishment of entire populations by starvation. He put explosives in toys and shot entire town councils to death when he was enraged and didn't know who else to shoot. Saddam let his sadistic sons spend millions of dollars on whores and parties and stunning perversions while human beings starved to death nearby. He let hundreds of thousands slaughter each other for his farcical attachment to dead empires. These things he did while invoking the name of God.

Of all the reasons we should know these horrible details is that Saddam's reign—his crimes and his madness—became, however inadvertently, part of history's process of deliverance for the Kurds. It would be trite to say their sufferings were mere birth pangs. They were far more. Still, the ground upon which a new and miraculous Kurdistan arises is soaked in the blood of martyrs. Every blessing that has come to Kurdistan today—and is yet to come—was purchased by the hundreds of thousands who died in the days of Saddam.

We owe them gratitude. We owe them remembrance. And if this is true, we owe them remembrance, particularly, of Halabjah.

Fathers of Modern Kurdistan

JALAL TALABANI

It says much about Jalal Talabani that he has been referred to by the name "Mam"—the Kurdish word for "uncle"—since childhood. His father once had a dream of a late "Uncle Jalal" offering the gift of an apple. He named his son after the uncle in the dream and didn't mind that the honorific "Mam" came with the name even while his son was still a child. So, Jalal Talabani would be known among the Kurds as "Mam Jalal"—"Uncle Jalal"—while Massoud Barzani would be known as "Kak Massoud"—"Brother Massoud." This speaks of the decade and a half between the two men in age but also of their difference in style: Massoud the easy-going, more traditional, simpler man; Jalal the older man and perhaps the one more worldly wise and progressive in views. It has taken both men to secure modern Kurdistan.

Jalal was born in 1933 near the town of Koi Sanjaq. He studied law at the University of Baghdad but the machinations of the Iraqi government moved him quickly into the role of rebel leader. In the 1960s, he commanded battlefields and devised strategies for guerrilla operations. In the 1970s, he split from the Barzani leadership and founded the Patriotic Union of Kurdistan (PUK) while continuing to lead armed incursions against Iraqi forces, some of these launched from within Iran. By the 1990s, his skills as diplomat and negotiator led to a ceasefire with the Iraqi Baathist government and to the establishment of Kurdistan as a safe haven under a U.S., French, and British secured no-fly zone.

He was more left leaning than other Kurdish leaders and often used terms like "our Comrades in China" or "the soviet of the Kurdish people." This did not endear him at first to a United States engaged in a Cold War with the Soviet empire. He learned, though, and he grew. His gifts became such that he was elected President of Iraq on April 6, 2005, after the fall of Saddam Hussein and Baathist rule. It has meant much both to the Kurds of Kurdistan and of the world that their Mam Jalal should be the first president of an independent and free

Iraq. Though ill health has plagued him in recent years, Kurdistan will be forever in the debt of Jalal Talabani. He and Massoud Barzani have formed something of the whole of leadership that a newly freed people have needed in order to create the Kurdish Miracle now celebrated around the world.

CHAPTER 7

HALABJAH

*"Nothing prepared me for the town of Halabjah, a community
that has the same resonance for the Kurds as does the Warsaw
Ghetto for the Jews or Guernica of the Basques."*
—Christopher Hitchens[1]

The road to freedom for an oppressed people seems always to require the defining violent episode. We can wish this weren't true, but history is too full of examples to deny the principle. The terrible moment seems to serve a purpose. It becomes not only a monument to the oppression of a people but also the galvanizing experience necessary for their deliverance. Black South Africans have their Soweto. Native Americans have their Trail of Tears or Wounded Knee. African Americans have their thousands of lynchings. India has its Amritsar. So the pattern continues.

The Kurds have their episode too: Halabjah. As long as Kurds live upon the earth, so too will the memory of

Halabjah. It was the event that reached beyond the censorship of Saddam Hussein's regime to a watching, horrified world. It was the event that exposed the complicity of Western nations with one of the most evil of history's regimes. It was the event that made undeniable the years of the Kurdish genocide that had already occurred—long before Saddam Hussein rained hell upon Halabjah.

We should remember also the evil irony of war that those who wear no uniforms and wield no weapons suffer most. The civilians, the townspeople, the non-combatants—they take the brunt of the conflict. They are punished for what armies do and then they rise the next day and try to live out normal lives. Their lands are ravaged. Their sons are taken. Their daughters abused. Their goods are confiscated in the name of someone's noble cause. They die—sometimes while they cook a meal or nurse a child. They suffer most in wars, and usually while both sides insist they are fighting the war just for them—the people who wear no uniform and wield no weapons.

The Iran/Iraq War was a glaring example of this irony. It was a vicious war of Islamic brothers in which entire civilian populations were held hostage, villages were bulldozed, and armies routinely slaughtered the innocent.

This was true the entire eight years of the war but it grew worse toward the end, at the beginning of 1988. Iran had successfully captured a number of Iraqi border towns and penetrated deep into Kurdish territory. Rather than oppose this incursion, the Kurdish Peshmerga, or guerrillas, took the risky step of opening a second front with Iranian support. They chose the city of Halabjah from which to launch this new front. As a Human Rights Watch report later explained, this tactic "only cemented the view of the Iraqi regime that the war against Iran and the war against the Kurds was one and the same thing." The results were devastating. Saddam Hussein had already declared his intent to wipe the Kurds from the face of the earth. This Kurdish/Iranian alliance gave him his opportunity.

Halabjah was a religiously conservative border town that served as a commercial center. It usually numbered forty thousand to fifty thousand people, but refugees fleeing the war had enlarged its population to over sixty thousand. The Iraqi regime watched the city closely. It was located just seven miles from Darbandikhan Lake and the dam that controlled much of the water needed in Baghdad. Halabjah could not be allowed to fall into Iranian hands. The regime held a tight rein as a result. Already, signs of local support for the Peshmerga had moved the regime to bulldoze two quarters of the city as punishment.

On March 13, the Iranians began shelling Halabjah to support the eventual attack. Iraqi troops quickly abandoned the outposts that dotted the area. This was a surprise and, in retrospect, should have served as a warning. Iraqi resistance was lighter than expected. This was unusual.

On the afternoon of the third day, the first Iranian car appeared on Halabjah's streets. By that evening, Iranians and Kurdish Peshmerga were walking the city openly. For the soldiers, there was a feeling of relief and celebration. Some rode motorcycles through the city and others ordered housewives to prepare them food. Some slept. Townspeople noticed that many of the Iranian soldiers were just boys and had only sticks and knives for weapons.

My friend, Nabard Sheik Mahmoud Al Naqshbandy, remembers the strange feeling in the town that day. "Everything was quiet. We knew that there had to be some counteraction coming from the Iraqi troops, but they were nowhere to be seen. We were nervous. The regime was not going to let the Iranians occupy such a strategic city. Something was wrong. It had happened too easily. There had hardly been a fight."

The people discussed leaving the city, but where should they go? The Iranians might think those who left the city were in support of Saddam. It would mean being shot. Some of the roads were closed due to fighting and spring flooding. None of this eased the fear. Nabard recalls, "we knew whatever the regime did was going to be bad, but we did not know what it would be."

The next morning, Iraqi planes began bombing. People ran to their makeshift shelters in basements and backyards. Halabjah had been bombed many times before, but this attack was different. It seemed the bombs were falling around the city, not on it. It was as though the explosions were intended to keep people from leaving Halabjah rather than destroy it.

This air assault continued into the afternoon and included napalm and phosphorous bombs. It was one of the most incessant attacks the people on the ground had ever seen. They recalled that there was no time to breathe between the groups of six planes that came one after the other.

Then, there was a short pause. The next sound came from the jets that began streaking overhead. Nabard remembers looking out of his kitchen window and seeing smoke to the north. It was not the smoke of a fire, though. It was low and dirty-white. It tended to move sideways rather than upwards. Nabard saw two children running about five hundred meters from where he stood at his window. Instantly, they both dropped to the ground. He knew they were dead. He also knew that the conventional bombing had ended and that Halabjah was being gassed. He yelled to his wife, grabbed his four-year-old child and ran to a neighbor's shelter.

Survivors recalled later the distinct smell. Some remembered it as the smell of garlic, others as rotting fruit or sweet apples. No one would forget it. Nor would they forget the moment they realized that the gas blanketing the town was heavier than air and was beginning to settle into the low places—which meant the crude shelters they had built themselves underground.

What those who were crammed into the dark and claustrophobic shelters could not have known at the time was that the Iraqi jets had dropped canisters containing four different types of gas, including mustard and sarin. Mustard gas burns the victim's skin with an agonizing sensation that often cannot be stopped. The burning continues in some cases for years. Sarin gas attacks the nervous system and usually kills within ten minutes. It is twenty-six times more powerful than cyanide. Those who do not die immediately begin suffering neurological damage that usually lasts the rest of their lives.

Saddam had dispatched the torments of hell upon Halabjah. Vicious chemical burns began appearing on skin. Eyes felt as though a thousand needles were piercing them. Many victims instantly went blind. The nose, mouth, and throat burned. Nothing brought relief. In seconds the gas attacked the lungs, which shut down and then started to liquefy. There seemed to be only two results for those who took in large doses of the gas. They either died instantly or they lived in the worst of torments and died later.

Mothers who smelled the gas and understood what was happening picked up their children and tried to run to safety. Seconds later, all were dead, their skin an ashen white, blood or foam spilling from their mouths. Some died so quickly it was as though they were frozen in time. Two women died trying to escape in their car, their bodies fixed in such natural positions that friends waved to them for days before realizing the women were dead. One woman died in her kitchen while cutting carrots. The knife never fell from her hand.

Some families sprinted for safety together and died almost in mid-air. Their bodies were haphazardly sprawled about the roads. Other small bands of family or neighbors seemed to understand the end had come and so they lay down in a final loving embrace. Members of medical teams who investigated later said they were haunted by the images of wives who had obviously died just as they were kissing their dead husbands.

When Nabard left his shelter for brief moments to see what was happening, he found scenes of chaotic insanity:

"People were running, screaming, crying—even tearing at themselves. The gas made some laugh hilariously. This was the strangest sight of all. Cars ran wildly through the streets. The living screamed out their grief for the dead."

Others recalled "Dead bodies—human and animal—littered the streets, huddled in doorways, slumped over the steering wheels of their cars. Survivors stumbled around, laughing hysterically, before collapsing ... those who had been directly exposed to the gas found that their symptoms worsened as the night wore on. Many children died along the way and were abandoned where they fell."[2]

Townspeople writhed on the ground in agony, ran wide-eyed with fear through the streets, or quickly went mad. Bodies lay everywhere. The gas made some victims vomit green bile and more than a few died with their faces frozen in terror at what spewed from their mouths.

People tried to protect each other. Two young boys suffocated to death in each other's arms, each having tried to cover the face of the other. Dozens of mothers died with their hands over their children's mouths in vain attempts to shield them from the gas. The bodies of fathers often concealed the children they had been trying to rescue. None had survived. Some parents were so preoccupied with trying to save their children that they did nothing to protect themselves. Severe burns made some faces unrecognizable.

In the days after, Iranian officials realized the importance of what had occurred and sent large groups of photographers. Some were European. This proved invaluable. Had no photographs been taken and no outsiders allowed to witness the scene, Iraqi officials would certainly have denied the atrocity ever occurred. They had done it before. With no evidence to confirm the horror, this act of genocide might have been dismissed as yet another imagining of excitable Kurds. Thankfully, hundreds of photographs provide undeniable proof.

One photo in particular has come to symbolize the anguish of that day in Halabjah. It depicts a Kurdish man who died at the doorstep of a neighbor, his son in his arms. The image is so gripping that it was cast in bronze and made part of the national memorial to the genocide. The description of how the man and his son came to be on that doorstep has nearly become the epitaph over Halabjah.

Uncle Omar had eight daughters and only one son, an infant, the last born. When the Iraqis began bombing Halabjah with chemical bombs, Uncle Omar took his most precious child—the little boy—and ran away from his house to a neighbor's shelter; but he couldn't make it and died on the doorstep of the neighbor's house, holding his baby in his arms. What Uncle Omar never knew was that he had no chance anyway.

All the members of the family who had gone to the shelter also died. The primitive shelter dug in their courtyard did not stop the deadly gases.[3]

The bombings ended late in the afternoon but the effects of the gas did not. The gasses continued to slither, settle, and kill. There was a residue that settled on every object and it could still contaminate and wound. A few photographers who visited the site weeks later made the mistake of touching clothing on which mustard gas had settled. They felt the burn instantly and required medical care. An unusual number of those who visited Halabjah after the gassing died of cancer.

While the victims continued to endure all the tortures Saddam intended, darkness fell. Those who could think clearly remembered that the Iranian bombings had knocked out electrical power. They could not stay in Halabjah. They needed hospitals. They needed food. They would freeze if they remained. As troubling, who knew when the planes would return or Iraqi ground troops would swoop in to deal with the living.

A long march to the Iranian border, which lay ten miles away over high mountains and through deep snow, became the only option. It would be a death march. Children and the elderly froze to death in the snow if they did not die of the gas already in their bodies. Adults who had helped others and trudged through the snow with heavy loads collapsed suddenly as their organs simply shut down. Some seven thousand died in the days after the attack, well beyond the five thousand who died during the hours of the attack itself. This was the genius of chemical weapons: they continued to kill long after first exposure.

Kurdwan Sheik Mahmoud Al Naqshbandy is today the Vice President of the Kurdish Military Supreme Court. He was twelve years old when the gas fell on Halabjah. But he was not there. His father, Nabard, and three brothers were. Kurdwan was in Sulimaniya when he heard of the attack. He raced to a mountain from which he could look down upon Halabjah. Using binoculars, he could see the chaos in the streets. He saw the insane and the blind and the dead. He also saw the Iranian soldiers, who had taken the city just a day before, now leaving the city and returning to Iran protected by their gas masks.

He could not make his way into the city. What would he do even if he could? He watched from his distance and worried for his father and brothers. Were they among the dead? Were they among those he saw laughing insanely in the streets?

Kurdwan's father, Nabard, had spent six hours in a crude shelter. It felt, he says now, like six years. A description of a similar shelter gives some sense of what Nabard endured: "Down in the shelter we huddled together in a corner, motionless and silent, our heads buried in our laps, until the sound of the planes had gone. There were nearly a hundred people down there all trampling on each other and the air was suffocating. Small children were screaming and crying . . ."[4]

Nabard decided it was time to leave the city. He loaded his wife and small children into his car and tried to leave by several of the usual roads. He realized that the Iraqi bombs that fell around the city earlier in the day were not just intended to bottle people up within the city, they were also designed to destroy roads and bridges that would allow escape after the attacks were over. This meant the Iraqis might return. Nabard knew that his only way of escape was toward Iran.

He moved his car onto the main road, turned east, and joined the great migration of human beings hoping for rescue in Iran. He could see panic just beneath the surface of the faces. Trucks, tractors, motorcycles, and cars of every size moved slowly along with those who were on foot. Some carted their dead in wheelbarrows. People seemed numb.

The gas continued to work. Many suffered diarrhea but could do nothing about it. Occasionally, a scream of grief told Nabard that another loved one had died, that another dead child was set tearfully by the side of the road, most likely by its mother.

In time, the road became too clogged to drive. It was time to walk. The climb over the mountains would begin anyway. Nabard put his child on his shoulders and told his wife to walk ahead of him so he could keep her in view.

A journey of slightly more than ten miles took three days. They were tired and hungry. They walked, they rested, they picked themselves up and walked on through snow and up steep mountains where often there were no roads. They knew that to leave the road was to risk the landmines Saddam had dropped all along the Iranian border. Each step could kill. When they weren't worrying about the mines, they wondered if they had absorbed enough gas to kill them. They worried, too, that Saddam's aircraft might massacre the long lines of refugees trudging toward Iran. More gas canisters could yet fall from the sky.

Finally, they saw Iranians coming to help them. They were taken to buildings that had been converted into hospitals. Nabard remembers the screaming of those whose bodies burned and would continue burning. He remembers the constant toll of the dead.

He and his family were driven to an Iranian town further into the interior. Other than being hungry and exhausted, he and his family were well. After a few days Nabard was eager to reclaim his car. He left his family in Iran and walked the twenty miles back over the mountains to the place he had left his car. He started the walk with bags of his family's clothes and goods, but he found he was too weak carry them the entire distance. He left the bags for others to find and made his way slowly, painfully to his car. It was intact but drained of gas. Someone had siphoned what fuel remained for their own journey to safety. Nabard found gas, drove north, and fell into the arms of the rest of his family. His wife and child rejoined him from Iran and they began to rebuild their lives.

When human rights organizations or Kurdish officials attempt to communicate the extent of the suffering in Halabjah and in the years afterward, they usually rely on a torrent of statistics. This is understandable. They wish to make their appeal with science, not emotion, and they wish to record what happened in the detail it deserves and that will last through time. This approach can leave a tragedy-weary world numb, though. It can even feel a bit clinical. Perhaps one day a history of Halabjah or a novel or perhaps a skillfully crafted documentary or movie will communicate what nothing but the silent photographs have been able to capture thus far of the madness and the indescribable pain.

Still, difficulty of description should not prevent the attempt, particularly when remembering Halabjah.

The truth is that the gassing of Halabjah continues to this day. The soil is too contaminated to use for agriculture and will be for years. Animals who feed in the area produce deformed young and die with tumors choking their organs. The descendants of survivors, even descendants of those who were not in Halabjah, but lived in the nearby region at the time, are plagued with sterility, infertility, cancers of every kind, birth defects, blood diseases, insomnia, depression, mental disorders, and a host of phobias. The social disruption produced by the attack led to declines in education, literacy, economic development, and political stability.

The toll in human suffering cannot be measured. Christopher Hitchens visited Iraq in 1991 and received a disturbing lesson in what Saddam's chemicals could do. A woman who had survived March 16, 1988, in Halabjah remembered, "I saw the planes come. I saw the bombs fall and explode. I tried to get out of town, but then I felt a sharp, burning sensation on my skin and in my eyes." She then astounded Hitchens by displaying her wounds: "Without warning, she drew up her voluminous dress and exposed her naked flank. Her whole left side, from mid-calf to armpit, was seared with lurid burns. And they were still burning."[5] Aside from the physical toll she had sustained, she also lost twenty-five members of her family in the Iraqi attack.

She is but one woman. There were twelve thousand who died as a direct result of the attack. Hundreds more have died in the years since. And this is but one attack of the many *Al-Anfal* massacres. These in, turn, are a small part of the murders committed by the Iraqi regime of Saddam Hussein.

We can focus on the blame. There was much to go around. The United States was so intent upon punishing Iran for a variety of offenses that it clung desperately to Saddam as an ally, armed him, turned a blind eye to his mistreatment of the Iraqi people, and even allowed American companies to sell the tyrant the tools he used on that day in 1988. The Kurds had no hearing in other capitals of the world, either, particularly in those nations whose corporations also had lucrative arms deals with Saddam.

There have been successful lawsuits and criminal prosecutions related to Halabjah. Saddam's cousin, Ali Hassan al-Majid, also known as "Chemical Ali," was hanged for his orchestration of the genocidal *Al-Anfal*. Others have been imprisoned. There is likely no end to the blame to be placed.

We must remember Halabjah but we must not live forever in Halabjah. A new Kurdish world is dawning and it began with an act that grew directly from Halabjah. In 1991, United Nations Security Council Resolution 688 established a no-fly zone above the 36th parallel of Iraq. It meant that no Iraqi planes could bomb villages or gas cities or strafe villagers on fire-lit hills. It meant that Kurdish children no longer urinated on themselves when they heard planes overhead. It meant that a helicopter landing in a field near a village might contain medical help or food or British engineers taking readings for a new water well.

It gave the Kurds an opening, and they took it. What is arising now in Kurdistan is the result of Kurdish genius given opportunity by American and European fighter jets and all of it inspired by the sacrifices of the martyrs. Finally, after all the suffering, the Kurdish Moment has come.

CHAPTER 8

MORE THAN MOUNTAINS FOR FRIENDS

"Saddam . . . had himself photographed, and painted on huge murals, in the robes of a mullah. He ordered that the jihadi slogan Allahuh Akbar ("God is Great") be added to the national flag of Iraq. He began an immense mosque-building program . . . He had a whole Koran written in his own blood . . . An Iraqi bounty was officially and openly paid to the family of any Palestinian suicide bomber. Yet none of this—including the naming of the slaughterhouse-campaign against the Kurds after a sura of the Koran—would unconvince the utterly smug Western "experts" who kept on insisting that his Caligula regime was a secular one."

—Christopher Hitchens[1]

It was 1988 and Jackson Harris was eager to meet a Kurd. He had heard of them. He had seen pictures. At the urging of his Presbyterian pastor, he had even been praying for them. He had yet to meet one, though. In fact, he and a small band of friends from church had become so desperate to cross the path of a Kurd that they occasionally spent evenings roaming the streets of Nashville in search of one.

I was moved as I listened to my friend describe his love for a people he did not know. This meant all the more to me because of the deep respect I have for Jackson Harris. He is not a spiritual oddball, not the gushy, overly emotional type of Christian so common today. He is, though, an unusual blend. He is a highly educated man and one of Nashville's finest artists. He is a keen mind and a tender soul, each revealed in his soft-spoken, southern manner and his deeply expressive, almost sad eyes.

"It was not hard to feel something for the Kurds in those days," Jackson remembers. "The Kurds were being forced into the mountains by the hundreds of thousands. The photographs were everywhere in the media. But we were feeling something beyond just human compassion for an oppressed people. We had this sense from God that our destiny was somehow intertwined with these people. Yet we had never even met a Kurd! It was odd and exciting all at the same time."

In the years Harris refers to, the phrase "10-40 Window" was popular among American churches. Coined by South American missiologist Louis Bush, the "10-40 Window" was used to describe the region of the world that lay between 10 and 40 degrees north of the equator. According to Bush, within this window existed some of the worst poverty in the world. It was also the region least influenced by the Christian gospel. Missionaries had long dubbed this region "the resistance belt," because it was populated mainly by Muslims, Hindus, Buddhists, animists, Jews, or atheists and had little Christian presence.

The 10-40 Window became a rallying cry to Christian missions both in North America and around the world. Numerous Christian ministries and denominations urged churches to focus upon the 10-40 Window in prayer, teaching, and missions giving. Prayer guides that described the various tribes of the region were widely distributed. Christians were urged to "adopt" one of these tribes—to learn about them, pray for them, and serve them. There were books, audio series, video courses, and conferences all designed to urge comparatively wealthy and comfortable North American Christians to invest themselves in this most poverty-ridden, war-plagued part of the world.

This is what moved Jackson and his friends to focus on the Kurds. As they prayed for the 10-40 Window, they felt their hearts drawn to the beleaguered people of Kurdistan. Yet, they were embarrassed by their ignorance. They knew almost nothing about the Kurds. While some of Harris' friends scoured local libraries for information, others scanned newspapers for the few details that seeped through reporting about Saddam Hussein and his designs upon Kuwait. Not satisfied with merely reading about the Kurds, the group would sit for hours in Middle Eastern grocery stores hoping they might see someone who looked like the photos in their prayer guides and in the *National Geographic* articles they had mined for information.

It was just then that news of Halabjah reached American newspapers. This moved the relatively few Kurds in Nashville to stage a protest against the atrocity in front of the federal courthouse in downtown Nashville. One of Harris's friends happened by this protest. Soon after, she called him. "I found one!" she nearly screamed into the phone.

A call to the local television station that had aired the protest story led to information about a leading Kurdish family. This was the connection the group had been waiting for. Soon, they befriended the Kurdish family and met still other families in the Nashville Kurdish community.

It was a small breakthrough but it was long sought and much prayed for. It would lead, in time, to the rise of one of the most effective Christian efforts in service of the Kurds. That this breakthrough occurred when it did seemed providential to Jackson Harris. Just then, the Kurds of Kurdistan were living through a hellish season. It was a time in which Kurdish desperation was giving way to despair, when the international community was largely ignoring the Kurds' cry for help and it was becoming increasing conceivable that the Kurds of Kurdistan might be wiped from the earth and that not a cry of protest would be heard the world over.

Few would have predicted in those days that the very crisis the Kurds then found themselves in would ultimately lead to a dramatic restoration of their homeland.

While Jackson Harris and his friends eagerly searched for Kurds on the streets of Nashville, Jalal Talabani, head of one of the two dominant Kurdish political parties of Kurdistan, searched eagerly for any sign of compassion in the capitals of the world. It was June of 1988. The flesh of Halabjah survivors was still burning—as it would in some cases for a decade more. More than a hundred thousand human beings had been killed in Saddam's *Anfal* against the Kurds. Talabani was hoping someone in the West would care.

The man who had engineered the atrocity of Halabjah and dozens more like it was Ali Hassan al-Majid, later dubbed "Chemical Ali" for his gas attacks on civilian populations. Prior to Halabjah, Ali was heard to say in a secretly recorded phone call, "I will kill them all with chemical weapons! Who is going to say anything? The international community? [Forget] them. The international community and those who listen to them."[2]

Jalal Talabani had not heard these words, but he knew their impact. In June of 1988, he traveled to London and then to Washington with a large white book listing the three thousand villages destroyed in Saddam's *Anfal*. The despot would not be satisfied with Halabjah, Jalal warned. He must be stopped.

It was true.

Though many in the West concluded Halabjah was little more than a final atrocity in the Iran/Iraq War of atrocities, Saddam soon went even further. The Iran/Iraq War officially ended on August 20, 1988. Yet on August 25, Saddam launched the final phase of his still incomplete genocide. His troops killed several thousand more Kurds in the Barzani heartland and then broke into the mountain valleys to demolish another seventy-seven villages.

An eight-year-old, who was tending the family livestock when her village was attacked, later remembered the horror of a bomb dropping near her house.

It made smoke, yellowish-white smoke. It had a bad smell like DDT, powder they kill insects with. It had a bitter taste. After I smelled the gas, my nose began to run and my eyes became blurry and I could not see and my eyes started watering too ... I saw my parents fall down with my brother after the attack, and they told me they were dead. I looked at their skin and it was black and they weren't moving. And I was scared and crying and I did not know what to do. I saw their skin turn dark and blood coming out of their mouths and from their noses. I wanted to touch them but they stopped me and I started crying again.[3]

The Iraqi troops had learned the lessons of Halabjah. No longer would they foolishly leave dead Kurdish bodies on the ground for the foreign press to photograph. On August 29, Iraqi forces gassed 2,980 fleeing Kurds to death in Bazi Gorge. This time, though, these troops stopped their ghastly rampage long enough to burn the bodies. They would prove Chemical Ali right. What would the international community do? How would they even know?

Try as he might, Jalal Talabani and other Kurdish emissaries could not move the Western powers to intervene. The U.S. government was particularly stubborn in its refusal to help, for it was far too intent upon the destruction of Iran to notice the atrocities taking place in Saddam Hussein's Iraq. Though U.S. armament companies sold weapons to both sides in the Iran/Iraq conflict, the

U.S. government had unquestionably favored Iraq. It was well-known, for example, that the Pentagon routinely gave Saddam satellite targeting information during the war to help Iraqi forces destroy Iranian installations. The U.S. was determined to see the defeat of the nation that had humiliated America by holding U.S. hostages in Tehran for more than a year. The price of this meager victory was feigning ignorance of Saddam's decade-long genocide against the Kurds.

Thus, Washington slammed the door in the faces of pleading Kurdish diplomats in a way that is shameful to recall these years later. Kurdish leaders with long-standing appointments at the State Department found themselves conducting their meetings on sidewalks across the street. Meetings with high-ranking officials were cancelled without explanation. Orders from the White House had been clear: do not be seen showing support for the Iraqi Opposition. This, of course, meant the Kurds.

Disappointments mounted. A "Prevention of Genocide Act of 1988," urged largely by Senator Claiborne Pell, was killed off by congressional disinterest and the weight of sanctions. A delegation of Kurds promised an appointment with senior State Department officials found themselves waiting for more than an hour before several minor officials scurried them out of the building to a nearby coffee shop. Only then would they hear the case the Kurds had come to plead. Meanwhile Saddam continued gassing Kurdish villages.

This callous dismissal continued from the fall of 1988 through July of 1990. Without support from the international community, Kurdish leaders could envision the total annihilation of their people. What Hitler had attempted, Saddam would do—the complete obliteration of a hated race. The world would allow it to happen. When Massoud Barzani proclaimed, "The Kurdish question is a political question which cannot be solved by military means," he was virtually declaring surrender. *We will almost certainly lose this war,* he was suggesting, *but it will not decide the Kurdish issue. That must ultimately be determined by the governments of the world.*

It was just then that a painful process of salvation began for the Kurds. On August 2, 1990, Saddam Hussein—pressing a longstanding case for Iraqi control of Kuwait and horribly misjudging the resolve of the U.S. and its allies—ordered Iraqi forces into Kuwait. This proved the awakening of the West. After much saber rattling and posturing, a Hundred Hours War drove the Iraqi army from Kuwait and focused the hopes of many Americans upon a change of governments in Baghdad. Finally, the West was paying attention. The national mood toward Saddam in the U.S. changed almost completely. No longer was Saddam a "good tyrant" the United States could use for its purposes. Instead, the man was evil, most Americans began to believe, and should be removed.

This is what President George H. W. Bush meant to call for in a speech on February 12, 1991. Speaking from the Old Executive Office Building in Washington, the president surprised his aides by suddenly going off-script. As he later described in his memoirs, Bush "impulsively added" the following words to his broadcast: "There's another way for the bloodshed to stop, and that is for the Iraqi military and the Iraqi people to take matters into their own hands and force Saddam Hussein, the dictator, to step aside."[4]

This was the scenario most Americans wanted, but it was not understood as clearly in Iraq as President Bush intended. As Quil Lawrence has written in his *Invisible Nation: How the Kurds' Quest for Statehood Is Shaping Iraq and the Middle East,*

It was the beginning of what would be called the "one bullet" policy. Washington wanted a kinder, gentler Sunni Arab general to blow off Saddam's head and then put Iraq and its oil back online for the world. But Bush failed to clarify that nuance, and his remarks were rebroadcast on the BBC, the Voice of America, and the CIA's propaganda transmissions to Iraq. Regular Kurds and Shi'ite Arabs heard it as a clarion call to rebellion.[5]

Almost immediately uprisings began in Iraq. The Shi'ites rose in revolt in southern Iraq, the Kurds in the north. By the middle of March, Duhok, Erbil, Sulimaniya, and Zakho had fallen to rebel forces. It was a thrilling moment. A popular uprising stirred by the words of the American president and encouraged by the mass desertions of Iraqi troops was sweeping the country. Massoud Barzani admitted, "The uprising came from the people themselves. We didn't expect it."[6] One spokesman explained that the Kurdish leaders had "merely followed the people onto the streets."[7]

There were other Kurdish victories but they were short-lived. The international coalition that had shoved Saddam's troops from Kuwait refused to then drive him out of Baghdad. He was still in power, still well-armed by Western weapons manufacturers, and still enraged by the Kurds when the uprisings began. Recriminations were rapid and merciless. Almost immediately five thousand women and children were taken hostage near Kirkuk.

Soon after, matters grew worse. The U.S. openly assured Turkey and Saudi Arabia that it would support neither the Kurdish nor the Shi'ite uprisings in Iraq. Then came an even more disastrous announcement. Washington declared that it would not forbid Saddam to use helicopters under terms of a cease-fire. There could hardly have been better news for Saddam Hussein, who had already received an astonishing gift in being allowed to stay in power. Now, he was free to vent his fury upon the offending Kurds and all while the U.S. stood by silently.

As the United States and its allies should have expected, the old atrocities began again. By the end of March, Iraqi troops had trained heavy artillery and airpower upon the rebels. Some one hundred thousand Kurds were captured within days with more than twenty thousand reported dead.

Panic spread. An estimated 1.5 million Kurds fled their homes in a "mad stampede" toward Iran or Turkey. Roads clogged nearly to a standstill. This was the signal Iraqi pilots had been told to wait for. Refugees who could not move for the press of bodies on the roads soon heard a familiar sound: the drumming rotors of Saddam's helicopters. Within minutes, the crews in these choppers began dropping phosphorous bombs upon the helpless and unsuspecting civilians. The horror of these bombings was staggering. One journalist reported seeing five hundred fleeing Kurds killed instantly by these bombs. "People are burned to death inside cars," he wrote. "Iraqi helicopters are bombing civilians without letup."[8]

Kurdish leaders understandably blamed the American president for inciting the uprising and then refusing to support it. Both Barzani and Talabani boldly and publicly criticized Bush. "You personally called upon the Iraqi people to rise up against Saddam Hussein's brutal dictatorship," they accused.[9] White House officials countered that there had been a tragic misunderstanding. Both were right, though the U.S. bore the greater responsibility for failing to understand some of the critical aspects of Kurdish culture.

Bush had intended to incite a single dissident soldier to kill Saddam and free Iraq of his madness. The Kurds, however, are a communal people who live in terms of covenant, loyalty, tribe, unity in the face of a common enemy, and unswerving devotion to friends. If George H. W. Bush, the American president, asked the Kurdish people to finish off the tyrant whom an international coalition had already driven out of Kuwait, the Kurds would be honored to do so.

They assumed, though, that the Americans would help. They assumed the United States would not allow a defeated madman to use helicopters and chemical weapons against unprotected civilians—again! And they assumed the U.S. government would not call for an uprising against a dictator only to entrench the man even more fully in power soon afterward.

The Kurds assumed—and they died ghastly deaths by the thousands for their assumptions.

Some two hundred fifty thousand Kurds fled through the mountains to the Turkish border. Despite the fact one of the worse snowstorms in Kurdish memory was just then beginning and despite the fact most of the Kurds left home in terror with little preparation for their arduous journey, the Turks callously closed their border. One journalist reported, "Mothers carrying babies confronted Turkish troops… begging to be allowed through to seek medical assistance… others brought grandparents on their backs or carried in makeshift stretchers of blankets. But anyone who tried to cross into Turkey was beaten back with rifle butts."[10]

By contrast, the Iranian government opened its borders to seventy-five thousand exhausted, terrorized Kurds and allowed its own Kurds to open homes, schools, and mosques to the exiles. Before long, refugee camps were built for some one million people. As exemplary as these humanitarian efforts by the Iranian government were, thousands of Kurds nevertheless died of exposure, dysentery, and exhaustion.

Photographs showing tens of thousands climbing steep, icy mountain roads filled the newspapers and magazines of the world. The sufferings of the Kurds were no longer deniable. Two-page spreads in national magazines revealed hundreds of burned, butchered bodies strewn upon snowy ground. The images reminded many Americans of photographs of their own Civil War.

Beyond the cruelties of Saddam's troops and the appalling duplicity of Western politicians, it is the courage of newspaper editorials we ought to remember from this time. A single paragraph from Britain's *The Independent* captures the righteous indignation reflected in hundreds of such editorials.

Mr. Major, to his shame, says he cannot recall asking them [the Kurds] 'to mount this particular insurrection,' as though the revolt were a freakish event which had nothing to do with us...The man [Bush] who reportedly told the CIA in January to provoke the Kurds into insurrection and preached rebellion during the Gulf War, now acts like someone with a nasty bout of amnesia.[11]

These editorials are important to recall because they forced action that had been far too long in coming. On April 5, the United Nations Security Council passed Resolution 688 condemning "the repression of the Iraqi civilian population in many parts of Iraq, including most recently in Kurdish populated areas" and it demanded, "that Iraq, as a contribution to removing the threat to international peace and security in the region, immediately end this repression [and] that Iraq allow immediate access to international humanitarian organizations to all those in need of assistance in all parts of Iraq."

Astonishingly, this was the first time the UN had mentioned the Kurds by name since the days of the League of Nations in the 1920s. It was the also first time the UN had insisted upon the right of interference in the internal affairs of a member state. So horrible had the Kurdish sufferings become.

While Saddam Hussein massacred Iraqi Kurds and the governments of the Western nations seemed eager to confirm that the Kurds were indeed a people without a friend, help did come for the Kurds, and it came from an unexpected quarter. It came from the compassionate in Frankfurt and London and Seoul. It came from Dallas and Detroit and Nashville. It also came from Jerusalem and Amman and Johannesburg.

This help did not come from governments. It came instead from those determined to defy their governments to serve a hurting people. Soccer moms and businessmen and pastors and bands of students—all moved by a sense of mission and those horrible photos of dead Kurds upon the ground—decided to do what their governments would not do and care for the needs of the devastated Kurds.

It was a movement comprised of people like Jackson Harris, who was just beginning to understand how desperate the needs of the Kurds truly were. Already he and his church had befriended the Kurdish community in Nashville. Already they had attended Kurdish picnics, learned Kurdish dance, picked up a bit of the Kurdish languages, and begun to love these gentle, gracious people beyond anything they had expected.

Then it happened. For years, Harris and his friends had prayed for the Kurds and learned all they could about their history. Now, the Kurds were beginning to flood into Nashville—courtesy of U.S. government relief efforts and the pleas of Nashville Kurds who had long made Tennessee their home.

"This was the beginning," Jackson explained. "When a network of Nashville churches began caring for the Kurds in the name of Christ, that's when things really began to take off. Dozens of volunteers began working to meet the most pressing needs of the Kurds who were just then pouring into Nashville: to learn English, learn to drive, secure a job, bring relatives to the U.S. from Kurdistan, and find places to meet with other Kurds in order retain their cultural identity. It was an exciting time, but it was also a lot of work!"

The turn few could have expected came from the pleadings of the Kurds themselves. Grateful as they were, they wanted their new American friends to help their kinsmen in Kurdistan. They were convincing. Their stories, the tears, the haunting memories, and the desperate needs were all poured out upon Americans like Jackson Harris. And this same immersion was repeated again and again, well beyond Nashville—in Detroit and Dallas, in Los Angeles and Atlanta and in hundreds of small towns across the U.S. So began a mobilization of aid from American churches and from people around the world that was as surprising as it was effective.

It was just as this groundswell began that I became involved in the cause of the Kurds. I was drafted by valiant men who were friends in those days and who were convinced that a once-in-a-generation opportunity was presenting itself. The "people without a friend" had been betrayed both by their Islamic brothers and by the international community. They were just then in agonizing need of nearly every essential of life. In the minds of my friends, the horrible state of the Kurds—who just might be the descendants of the ancient Medes—issued a mandate no serious Christian could ignore.

The efforts of compassionate souls from around the world on behalf of the Kurds was impressive. The stalwarts who drew me into helping the Kurds, for example, believed that the Christian Church worldwide was being given an opportunity to serve an entire people group and not merely to provide clothing and jobs to a few refugees. Some of these stalwarts were experienced statesmen. Some were medical professionals. A few were from America's Ivy League schools. Others were technicians or career missionaries. All understood that among a people so nearly decimated as the Kurds, aid would have to come in greater variety and at higher levels than usual.

The help extended to the Kurds during this time took on dimensions few missionaries or aid workers would have previously imagined. Even my relatively minor work on behalf of the Kurds was surprisingly multifaceted. To help with relief efforts, I traveled to Kurdistan perhaps a dozen times, met with men like Massoud Barzani and Jalal Talabani, and taught in Kurdish universities and as a PBS-style lecturer on Kurdish television. I was part of a team that informally lobbied Congress on behalf of the Kurds and that demanded Saddam Hussein be charged with war crimes. I was also part of a two-man team that traveled to the Vatican to ask for help in resolving Protestant/Catholic tensions in Kurdistan.

Comparatively, my work was nothing. Others I knew started clinics, built houses, planted churches, performed surgeries, raised millions of dollars, wrote books, and even founded businesses to fund work among the Kurds. One American doctor, then Air Force Colonel Jerry Brown, personally funded a computer-based medical resource center and oversaw the complicated and dangerous operation of backpacking the equipment into Kurdistan. This digital clinic allowed Kurdish doctors to keep abreast of medical advances denied them in Saddam Hussein's Iraq.

On our many trips into Kurdistan, we discovered organizations from European countries providing education for Kurdish children, an American Christian firm that dug wells to provide water for remote villages, faith-based British firms that supported removal of landmines, and a ministry from Scotland that distributed books and literature. The recovering Kurdish regional government welcomed it all.

To describe the efforts of Christians on behalf of the Kurds and the welcome these Christians received in Kurdistan is not to say that somehow the Kurds had abandoned their Muslim heritage. A drowning man will accept help from any source and there is no question the Kurds were drowning in the 1990s. Many faiths responded with aid, as did many nations. Yet there is an important truth of religion that played a role at the time, and I know my Kurdish friends will not be offended by its mention.

This truth is that in the years after the *Anfal* many Kurds were questioning their Islamic faith. It was not lost on them that much of their suffering had been at the hands of fellow Muslims. It did not escape their notice that Saddam Hussein seduced mullahs into issuing murderous *fatwas*—official religious decrees—and generally manipulated the Islamic faith to harm the Kurds. Indeed, the very name for the genocidal campaign against the Kurd, *Anfal*, was a word straight from the Koran! Saddam delighted in positioning himself as a righteous man when in fact he was no more a righteous Muslim than Adolf Hitler was a righteous Roman Catholic.[12]

It was natural, then, for Kurdish Muslims to distance themselves somewhat from traditional Islam and certainly from fundamentalist Islam in the early 1990s. Their faith had been used against them. Aid was coming largely from non-Islamic nations. Some of their most eager friends were the Christians of the world. It was no surprise to me that more than one Muslim friend asked aloud, "Have we been in darkness for fourteen hundred years?" He was referring to the centuries during which the Kurds had been under the sway of Islam and his question had more to do with Islam as a process of Arabization than it did Islam's teaching about Allah and righteousness. In other words, had the Kurds embraced a faith that eroded their Kurdishness and made them slowly into Arabs—when it was Arabs who had brought them so much grief? The torment in the faces of my friends as they pondered these questions was hard to see.

I often shared my Christian understanding of these issues with my Kurdish friends and they graciously welcomed my views. I could not resolve their tensions with Islam, though, and many were tormented by what they had experienced at the hands of their own faith for years after. Some still are.

What I could do—and I did it with delight—was to point out the all-important change in the fortunes of the Kurds that had occurred. They were no longer a people without a friend. They no longer had only silent mountains to look to for comfort. I could figuratively sweep my hand over their land and point out workers from nearly every country and faith all laboring to serve the Kurds in perhaps their darkest hour.

I could tell stories of the family of nine in Columbia, Tennessee, that kept a "Kurd Jar" on their dining room table in which to gather money for Kurdish relief. I could describe a college student in London who spent time learning Kurdish languages on top of his already-heavy academic load. He did this in hope of one day serving the Kurds of Kurdistan. I often described the engineers in Germany laboring on new technologies with the thought of helping to restore Kurdistan specifically in mind. I could also movingly describe the Buddhist monk who had decided that Koreans could help solve the challenges Kurds faced removing landmines. They might risk their lives, but they had determined to set themselves to dismantle this evil fruit of an evil regime.

Whatever the Kurds would become as a people, whatever they might choose to believe, and however the governments of the world might choose to treat them, they were no longer alone. Their cause had become the cause of generous, compassionate souls around the world—and this time they would not be forgotten.

CHAPTER 9

THE GENIUS
OF THE KURDS

"When we disembarked on free soil at the
Erbil Airport, there was a group of Kurds waiting
to greet me as a friend and ally and I felt
at that moment as if my boy might feel that
his old father had not been entirely a jerk."

—Christopher Hitchens[1]

The measure of a people's true greatness is often revealed in what they do when their day of freedom comes. This has certainly been true of the Kurds and what they have done since freedom began to dawn for them in the summer of 1991.

When the agonies of the Kurds could no longer be ignored—after even the U.N. had reached its limits and demanded its member nations intervene to halt the Kurdish genocide—the Western military powers were finally forced to act. This came first in the form of a no-fly zone over northern Iraq.

Named Operation Provide Comfort—and then, later, during the Clinton administration, renamed Operation Northern Watch—this was an effort by U.S., British, and French air forces to safeguard Kurdistan by keeping Iraqi aircraft from crossing the 36th parallel. It meant Saddam could not send gunships to strafe terrified Kurds and could not drop Sarin gas or phosphorous bombs upon the innocent and the helpless. This no-fly zone was so successful that the next year Operation Southern Watch was established to protect Iraq's Shi'ite population in the south of Iraq.

It was a meager mercy. It was far from all the West could have done but it was the least of what it ought to have done. Had the U.S. and its coalition allies allowed Saddam Hussein's government to continue exterminating Kurds, they risked not only losing the glory of victory from the recent war, but also the damning judgment of history that they had betrayed the Kurds and thus betrayed their oft-touted principles. They had to act. Decency demanded it. Yet they were still unwilling to put troops in Kurdistan and involve themselves in the "internal affairs of Iraq." So they flew jets from Germany, Turkey, and Italy to protect the Kurds from the sky-borne terrors of Saddam Hussein.

It was a meager mercy, but it was enough.

As time would confirm, all the Kurds needed in order to take control of their destiny was a bit of relief from the unrelenting horrors visited upon them. They asked only that the West stop supporting those who would steal that destiny from them. They asked that their villages not be gassed in the night and that the flesh of their children not be set aflame by phosphorous bombs. They asked that those who called themselves allies not sell Saddam Hussein the gas that drove their elderly mad and paralyzed the lungs of their children. Give them this and they would care for themselves. They would do so despite a foolish civil war between their two dominant political parties. They would do so despite the starvation and disease they endured when international economic sanctions against Iraq failed to exclude them. They would do it despite yet another international war against Saddam on their soil.

This was all they asked. This, and perhaps that promises could be kept and betrayals kept to a minimum. Yes, that would help, too.

And so it began. The turning. With hell no longer raining from the skies after August of 1991, the Kurdish genius began to reveal itself. The region's leaders moved swiftly to secure their land. Slowly, unsteadily, Jalal Talabani and Massoud Barzani led the Kurds in rebuilding. In a general election the next year, the two men split the vote and thus split the various government ministries evenly. Tensions over this arrangement eventually led to armed conflict in 1994, but it also allowed the journey out of chaos to begin.

For older Kurds who had endured so much, this was a season to rest, to feel what it might mean to walk the streets as an almost free people. For the young, these were days of dizzying excitement.

Raz Rasool was a college student in her early twenties at that time. She remembers the thrill of being a Kurd in a Kurdistan just awakening as though from the dead. "It was such an exciting time," she recalls. "We had lived for so long just day to day. We could make no plans. We had no future. Always the control of our lives seemed to be in the hands of those who hated us." Then came the no-fly zone, that umbrella of protection intended to allow the Kurds to assume control of their own affairs. "We had nothing, but we were so excited our hearts were bursting. There were no tools, no money. But the spirit of the people was there. That's what I remember most. We were finally moving. We had never dreamed it might be possible."

It was all more than the Kurds had hoped. They were only four years from Halabjah, were even then enduring a suffocating double-embargo—international economic sanctions against Iraq exacerbated by Baghdad's internal sanctions against the Kurds—and always there was the *Anfal*. None of this was ancient history. It was only the year before that a million and a half Kurds had fled their land in terror during the worst winter in memory. Nothing had come easily, but now they could dream again—and plan.

Rasool volunteered at a variety of government offices, as many of the young and eager were doing in those days. Conditions were so spare that the words "government" and "office" barely applied. She worked in any empty space available. Often, she had to borrow vehicles to carry out the simplest errand. Ancient typewriters required that she type important reports and proposals again and again until she could produce a copy free enough of errors to send on. "But it was the spirit that kept us going. The spirit of the people," she recounted to me through tears. "We had our own country. For the first time in my life we could think about a future as a people."

Some Kurds serving with Rasool at that time of dizzying change remember it in terms of the American experience. Bizad, who works today as an engineer for an Oklahoma petroleum company, compares working distantly for Massoud Barzani in the 1990s to serving the Continental Congress during the American Revolution. "I know it is not the same," he says pleadingly, "but I thought of us as though we were giving birth to a new nation. I thought we were fighting—even with paper and pens, even with a government that no one recognized—as the pioneers of a new country. My friends and I used to joke with each other and call each other Jefferson or Washington or Adams. We thought we were revolutionaries overthrowing an evil king. In a way, I guess we were."

The efforts of old and young alike were eventually rewarded. Because a struggling government did all in its power to keep schools open, in 1992 the U.N. answered by providing teachers. This was an early and encouraging sign that the outer world would help rebuild Kurdistan and not limit their help to the no-fly zone.

Equally encouraging were the donations to the Kurdish cause that began pouring in. Money began arriving from all over the world in amounts large and small. A handful of coins arrived from a five year-old in California. Several million dollars were smuggled in from collections among the often-oppressed Kurds in Turkey. Even more encouraging were tens of millions of dollars sent by Jalal Talabani's wealthy relatives and friends in Europe.

Soon, international aid organizations began locating in the urban centers of Kurdistan and, when their efforts proved successful, multi-national corporations followed. This meant jobs and an increase in services.

As conditions improved and confidence began growing abroad that Kurdistan might be a promising market, a strategic partnerships became possible. This allowed for fledgling private firms to arise, firms that in time would become highly successful and contribute to the economic miracle just then underway.

Among the most notable of these was the company the world would eventually know as Asiacell. It was founded by Farouk Rasool, a cagey, wise, somewhat secretive man who combined raw courage with business savvy to both serve the technological needs of his people and to build one of the most successful tech companies in the Middle East. When the jets of the West finally provided a no-fly zone to protect the Kurds, he bought a $15,000 satellite device from Inmarsat Pic (ISAT) to create a call center in Sulimaniya. Four years later, Asiacell was born. We should remember that Saddam Hussein had long banned mobile phones in Kurdistan as a tactic to isolate and control the Kurds. Thankfully, Mr. Farouk was undaunted.

He also knew the art of the deal. In 2003, seven months after the second U.S. invasion of Iraq, he partnered with Kuwait's National Mobile Telecommunications Company and won a license to run a GSM wireless network in northern Iraq. Though at first the service was spotty—users needed separate mobile devices to make calls in the various regions of the country—the system improved over time.

Asiacell's record of success under Mr. Farouk's leadership is stunning. It became the first company to provide quality mobile telecommunications in Iraq and now has over 10 million customers. It provides service in all eighteen of Iraq's governorates, reaches 97 percent of the populace, and has become Iraq's leading brand, recognized the world over.

But it all began in those early days when a no-fly zone first gave the Kurds enough relief from bombardment for their native genius to arise. It was a gift, as was the removal of Saddam Hussein from power in 2003 and the flood of foreign aid and investment that entered the country as the world awoke to the economic possibilities of a newly liberated Kurdistan.

I was there in those days and what struck me most was the entrepreneurial spirit among the young. The Middle East has always been a locus of trade, barter, investment, haggling, and passion for profit. We read from our earliest school days of caravans and *souks* (bazaars), of Arab and Persian merchants and the finely crafted goods of the region but we rarely imagine what innate entrepreneurial gifts this might embed in each new generation.

The Kurdish version of these gifts, long stifled by war and economic isolation, came roaring to the fore particularly among the young of Kurdistan in the early years of the new millennium. It was as though the dreams of their fathers and grandfathers—dreams stillborn in those earlier generations—surged to freedom in the millennial generation of newly liberated Kurds.

Loving twenty-somethings of any nationality as I do, I sat for hours in schools and watering holes listening to the economic dreams of the first Kurdish generation in a hundred years for whom such dreams were more than fantasy. A young visionary named Besna, whose flashing brown eyes and flowing locks unhidden by a burka spoke of her ambition and pride, told me—in sentences almost too rapid for my interpreter, a Kurd with a doctorate in English—that she and her sister were planning to start a dress shop. An uncle owned a small commercial space that he had rented out, she explained, but he had promised to let his nieces have it rent-free for a few months to see what the girls could do. They would make it a success, Besna assured, and they would do it debt-free. They had been saving.

Ferhad, an exceptionally handsome twenty-four-year-old with a passion for technology, envisioned wealth coming his way from his ability to broker deals. At great length, he explained how he had often heard his father and brothers discuss connections they needed in business. He would listen carefully over dinners and then, the next day, he often arrived at the family business with the perfect client in tow. He had a gift. He knew it, and he intended to offer this gift to an international slate of clients. He would open an office and introduce firms to each other. He could see it in his mind's eye. More than once he erupted in the middle of his own stream of thought with a question about what connections I might need to be "even more a successful man, Mr. Mansfield. Think of it. An even more successful man."

And so it would go. I thought often of what great opportunities would come the way of this young generation once microfinancing firms like Kickstarter could take hold on Kurdish soil. Western financial mechanisms combined with Kurdish drive and ingenuity might well transform the Middle East—or at least Kurdistan.

My young entrepreneurially-minded friends surprised my investor friends in the United States because they emerged from a long, dark night of oppression and stepped into the brilliant light of freedom eager to succeed, eager to test themselves against the markets of the world, and certain about the pathways to prosperity and lasting stability.

I'm asked to explain this often and I attribute it to a wide variety of causes. First, we must remember that when the bombs were not falling and there was no need to rush to the mountains, Kurdish youth were watching Middle Eastern versions of FOX, CNN, MSNBC, BBC and SKY News, all of which articulated Western economic ideas to young minds. This rising generation also had websites and social media at hand. They interacted with youth around the world and fed from foreign dreams. They, too, followed rock stars whose great wealth set dreams to flight and led to serious thought about how capital might be used. Then there were the skills and strategies of their own heritage and all that the years taught about what did not work economically—Baathist socialism, for example—and what did.

The young were quick, smart, and eager. They listened. They learned. When opportunity came, they did not hesitate. Their destiny awaited and it was one with the destiny of their newly ascending people.

This young generation was also brilliantly led by their peoples' leaders. Nothing taught the core principles of economic prosperity like the astonishing "Investment Law of 2006." Of all the brilliant decisions that I have watched the Kurdish authorities make in pursuit of prosperity for their region, this law was the most astonishing and the most fruitful. I have seen nothing like it elsewhere and it is my view that much of the Kurdish economic dynamism celebrated today is a direct result of this daring decision.

We should remember that throughout the world there is a growing trend toward socialism. Few societies can be labeled strict capitalist societies and fewer still can be classified as libertarian. Protectionism, tariffs, ever-higher taxes, state intrusion in markets, and ever expanding public services are the rule. The philosophical children of John Maynard Keynes now prevail.

It is for this reason that the 2006 Investment Law of Kurdistan is so astonishing. In one great act, the

Kurdistan National Assembly passed—and regional President Massoud Barzani ratified—a law that put out the welcome mat to global investment in a manner that is now transforming the region and guaranteeing the continuation of the Kurdish economic miracle so touted today.

Among the many provisions of this law is first that foreign investors and indigenous investors are to be treated equally. Article 3 states that "Foreign investors and foreign capital shall be treated the same way as national investors and national capital." It concludes, "A foreign investor shall be entitled to own all the capital of any project that he sets up in the Region under this law."

This means, in effect, that anyone in the world with the means can start a business in Kurdistan and be treated under the law just as one who had lived in Kurdistan his entire life. The foreigner can start a business, own land, and invest with the same rights as any citizen of the Kurdistan autonomous region. This is an amazing break from the trend of the surrounding nations and, again, evidence that the Kurds are determined to set themselves apart. They might have emerged from their many battles for territory a grasping and self-preserving people. Instead, they set themselves to invite the world to the grand partnership of Kurdistan.

Another provision of this transforming legislative act was equally stunning. Article 4 of the Investment Law promises free or reduced-price land for most foreign investment projects. Another provision guarantees foreign investors complete rights to repatriate their profits in full. This means a foreign firm may invest in Kurdistan and then take all profits to its home country "in full." Few nations in the world are as generous.

The law also guarantees foreigners the same rights to own land for investment purposes as are given to those who live in Kurdistan. More astonishing still is the law's guarantee of a ten-year tax break for foreign investors once their company begins production or starts providing services. This same provision guarantees new ventures exemption from customs fees on imports for five years.

The genius of the Kurds in this law is obvious. As the new millennium dawned, Kurdish leaders took stock of their situation. They had little to offer but land, rights, and freedom. In typically Kurdish fashion, they offered these willingly to the world. *You are welcome. It will be an honor to us.* The result has been an influx of foreign investment that is transforming the once "flatlined" region into a rising first world economic model.

Yet the Kurds know that it takes more than laws to build a stable economy. The conditions surrounding that economic activity must also be conducive. Thus, the Kurds have set themselves to fashioning a just society and not merely a successful economic one. Consider these stunning facts.

- Kurdistan has one of the lowest tax rates in the world. This is largely due to the Kurdistan Regional Government's (KRG's) petroleum income, but it is also the result of an unswerving commitment by the KRG to keep taxes low. The average citizen in the Kurdish region pays only 1 or 2 percent of his income in taxes—if he pays any taxes at all!

- The more moderate version of Islam practiced in the Kurdish region grants greater freedom for women. Though women still have a huge distance yet to travel in acquiring the liberties women enjoy in much of the Western world, by the standards of the Middle East Kurdistan is an extremely welcoming environment. There are female Supreme Court justices, female entrepreneurs, females commanding Peshmerga units, female police officers, and females who head departments in the KRG. Women stroll the streets of Kurdistan without headscarves and do not fear reprisals. Their contribution to the Kurdish economic miracle is unquestioned.

- Kurdish leaders have also been careful to assure a stable security situation, as we shall see. While foreign companies flee the south, where bloodshed and corruption reign, Kurdistan is providing the type of secure environment in which business thrives.

- At the same time that the south of Iraq is suffering a tragic departure of Christians due to persecution and bigotry, most of these religious refugees make their way into Kurdistan, taking their education, skills, and international connections with them. Since 2003, more than fifteen thousand Christian families have been forced to flee the south of Iraq. Some have chosen to live in Europe, but most have settled in Kurdistan. In short, the largely Muslim Kurdish region is being careful to create a religious safe haven that will serve it well in the years to come.

- Finally, the Kurds understand the wisdom of a federal system. Though they are many times more prosperous than the south of Iraq and though many in Kurdistan are urging independence, the KRG has been temperate in this matter. It is not led by radicals. Instead, it is led by men who believe in each region of Iraq controlling its own destiny but as part of a mutually beneficial federation. As former Prime Minister Barham Salih explained, "We have studied the question of independence and concluded that the Kurdish region is best served as a loyal part of Iraq." If the Kurds do eventually declare themselves an independent nation, it will be because the government in Baghdad wishes to dominate rather than participate in a federal system that builds on the strengths of each region. The Kurds understand the virtues of such a system. Many of their leaders have been educated in the best universities in the West. They know of history as well as the lessons taught by the great economists of the world. By contrast, the government in Baghdad seems to have learned more from Baathist Nazi-style socialism than from the experiments of the free and prosperous nations.

What I have said above about conditions in Kurdistan—and what I am about to report—is shocking to my audiences. The reason is their confusion of the south of Iraq with the northern region in which the Kurds live. Nearly everyday people around the world hear bad news from Iraq and they assume that what is true in Baghdad—where most of the bad news emanates—is true of the entire country. It isn't. The difference between the Shi'ite-dominated federal government in the south run by Prime Minister Nuri al-Maliki and the semi-autonomous region of Kurdistan run by the Kurdistan Regional Government (KRG) in the north is as different as New York is from West Texas.

As recently as 2013, it was not uncommon for 50 people a week to die in the south of Iraq. Media reports in the United States often began with a statement similar to this: "More tragic deaths occurred today in Iraq." It was true but it wasn't the whole truth. Rarely were there any killings in the Kurdish region during this same time. To put this truth in perspective, consider that in September of 2013, six people were killed when terrorists detonated a bomb in a mini-bus at the gate to a police facility in Erbil. Prior to that tragedy—which shocked the peace-loving region— the most recent terrorist attack in Erbil had been six years prior in 2007. Before that, a bombing had occurred in 2005. In all, fifty people had died of terrorist acts in Kurdistan since 2005—an eight-year stretch. This was equal to one week in Baghdad in 2013. Clearly, the south of Iraq was not then and is not now the north of Iraq.

The economic difference between the two is also stark. While Prime Minister Maliki led the south into militarism, central economic planning, political chaos, and corruption of nearly every kind, the Kurdish region in the north is enjoying an economic growth rate of more than 10 percent and a Gross Domestic Product that is 50 percent higher than the rest of Iraq. While the south has driven investment away, the north has welcomed it, as we have seen. There are over 1,500 Turkish companies operating in the Kurdish region and dozens of multi-nationals like Exxon, John Deere, Chevron, Hilton, Marriott and Hunt Oil.

Torrents of stunning economic statistics pour from the KRG almost daily. There is a magnificent $550 million airport that increased traffic by a third in the single year between 2011 and 2012. Five- and six-star hotels open at a rate of at least one a year, and these are joined by increasing numbers of shopping malls, restaurants, office complexes, parks, hospitals, and grocery stores. A Lebanese firm has built a "Dream City" with western-style restaurants and a 1,200-room housing development. There is Naz City with shiny condominiums that would be envied in most cities of the world. The suburbs boast an English Village, an Italian Village, and an American Village with upscale homes that range to just under ten thousand square feet.

While numerous European corporations have stopped doing business in the south of Iraq due to corruption, violence, and economic instability, multinationals have pledged even greater investment in the north. Almost daily, a new project is announced with billions of dollars in future development intended. It is all promise that the Kurdish economic miracle will continue so long as Kurdistan retains its commitment to being a free, stable, safe, and just society.

It would be wrong of me, having so fully celebrated the accomplishments of my Kurdish friends, to fail to serve them by expressing also a few of my concerns. This is what friends do for each other—warn and question and even correct, as well as encourage—and I am, without apology, a friend of Kurdistan.

As much as I admire the gifts and noble intentions of Massoud Barzani and Jalal Talabani, I am concerned about continued control of Kurdistan by a few wealthy families.

As benevolent as their influence has been of late, I fear for the concentration of power into the hands of the few in any society and I hope that this feature of Kurdish society may dissipate. Kurdish leaders extol the virtue of an Iraqi and Kurdish republic. May this dream come quickly and completely.

I fear, also, that my Kurdish friends may not distinguish themselves sufficiently from the darker trends among their Islamic brothers. Honor killings—largely of women and largely over questions of freedom and modernization—are on the rise throughout the Islamic world. They are on the rise in Kurdistan too. This has potential to threaten all that lovers of Kurdistan today hold dear and all that Kurdish leaders hope the region may become. No true friend of Kurdistan could fail to say that this must be stopped and stopped completely. Laws against this must be firm and retribution by authorities swift and final. No society can be a great society and allow women to be murdered for the clothes they wear or the values they espouse.

I fear, also, that an effective banking system may remain out of reach for the KRG. It is the one great hindrance to a complete market economy that plagues the region now. This is within the hands of Kurdish leaders and it must become an urgent priority if the Kurdish Miracle is to continue.

Finally, I fear that the United States may continue to foolishly arm and support the Iraqi government in Baghdad, and thus, one day bear the guilt for a devastating and bloody invasion of Kurdistan from the south. Patriot that I am, I am nevertheless ashamed of my nation's repeated betrayal of the Kurds. They are true friends and ought to be among our dearest allies. The Kurds have wished this for nearly a century. It is time for the United States to make it so.

These fears for the land I love do not outweigh my confidence that Kurdistan's rise will last. I have given many reasons for this confidence in these pages, but there is one additional basis for hope I would offer, and it is the life of one man whom the Kurds have welcomed and who now has chosen to make Kurdistan his home. His name is Yousif Matti al Qas and he is one of the men I admire most in the world.

As great a man as he is, it is his laughter that comes to me most often when I think of Yousif. It constantly betrays him. When he intends a humorous comment, he cannot keep from giving himself away. His voice rises. He begins to shake. Sometimes he finds it hard to breathe. When he finally finishes the joke or funny story, he erupts in such intense laughter that it seems to possess him. Soon he is wiping his eyes with his handkerchief and shaking his head.

If he has been speaking in English, he will often then turn to someone in his family to tell it all a second time in Arabic. This is unnecessary, of course. His entire family speaks English better than I do. One of his daughters told me that her father does this just so he can experience the joy of a good laugh a second time.

It may seem odd to introduce someone primarily by their sense of humor, but when you have been in life-threatening situations with a man and have found comfort again and again in the sound of his laugh, it seems a gift from God. Yousif was present during many of the firsthand experiences I've described in this book. When our team got stuck on the wrong side of the Turkish/Iraqi border and PKK guerrillas opened fire, it was Yousif who piped up and said—while we hid behind concrete barricades—"we will get through this, but we will be late for dinner." It was a slight comment, but it meant the world to me at the time.

It was his son who kept getting into and out of my suitcase after an anti-Christian riot tore through the family's front door. Yousif had to be nearly undone by the panic he saw in the boy's eyes. He kept his faith, though, and trusted me a bit even when he saw me wrestling his son in the dirt and jokingly trying to tie him to a goat. When the child kept getting into and out of my suitcase, Yousif walked in the room and said, "Son, I could have bought you a suitcase for Christmas if that is what you wanted. It would have been much cheaper than all those toys!" Somehow, the boy understood in his father's levity that everything was going to be all right. Yousif's laugh always made me feel the same way.

Yousif Matti al Qas was born in June 1955 to a Roman Catholic family in Baghdad. His people were from Nineveh and were shaped more by that knowledge than they were by the culture of Baghdad. Yousif remembers that he grew up around informed, well-read, well-educated people.

This had its effect on him. From an exceptionally early age, he thought often about the merits of various governmental systems. He read Marx and Engels and discussed what he read with friends and the like-minded in his family. Clearly, he was wrestling with issues of justice and higher truth well before others of his age.

He attended college to study geology and prepare for a career in the petroleum industry. Then the Iran/Iraq War began. Like many other young men, Yousif was drawn into military service. Because he was a college graduate, he was chosen for advanced training as a radar specialist. This kept him from the fighting and left him with many long, uneventful hours.

He was sometimes required to serve guard duty and on these occasions, he often passed the numbing time by standing under the single light bulb available so he could read. What he read most was the Bible. It was not something he would have imagined himself doing earlier in his life. His brother-in-law, Mahir, had become a Christian a few years before and had begun urging the family to believe that Jesus Christ was alive and still changing lives as described in the New Testament. Yousif read the scriptures, prayed as Mahir said he should do, and, in time, he, too, felt he had been "saved" and become a follower of the Jesus who was still alive as he had been centuries ago.

He left the army in the early 1980s just as tensions were rising between the Iraqi government and the Kurds. Life kept Yousif busy, though. He had a wife, three small children, and a rising career to tend.

Despite their distractions, Yousif and his wife, Alia, could not escape the great suffering of the Kurds. Seeing the poor, the women widowed by war, the children hungry and abandoned—the scenes would not leave his mind. The images formed a kind of commission, he felt, but he wasn't sure how to fulfill it. What good could he do in helping the Kurds? How could a geologist be of any help? Still, he prayed and confided in his wife the things he was feeling. This was while the Kurds continued to starve and suffer and die from Saddam's evil.

Finally, Yousif and Alia came to a conclusion. God was calling them to serve the Kurds. They were certain that God wanted them to stand with the Kurds at that horrible time in their history.

They started by smuggling Bibles. Yousif built a false bottom in the family van and learned to pack the hidden space with Bibles that the family then drove across the border into Kurdistan. They were very successful and were never caught. Yet one day Yousif learned from fellow Christians who were well-placed in government that Saddam's security forces had learned about the smuggling. This placed the family in great danger.

Soon after, Yousif and Alia awakened their children late one night and told them they had to leave quickly. Noor, their oldest child, was only seven at the time. She remembers the constant changing of cars and that the family lived with numerous families in their effort to get safely to the Kurdish border. Finally, Noor remembers that she had been sleeping on a bus when she woke to see the beautiful mountains surrounding the Kurdish city of Duhok. She had never seen mountains or snow before.

The family searched for a home and finally learned of a house that seemed perfect but that no one would buy. The previous owners had been slaughtered in the house. People said it was haunted. The Mattis wouldn't let silly rumors keep them from what they saw as God's provision. They took the house, prayed in all the rooms, and settled in. Ghosts never troubled them.

They were troubled, though, by the desperate needs around them. The people were broken. Despair and disillusionment ruled. Everything was in short supply. There was much to do.

Yousif had never been trained for ministry. He only knew to do what he had seen the churches in Baghdad do. He taught the scriptures. He started a Sunday school program. He gathered young people into his home and tried to make spiritual things relevant to youths living in a war-torn land. None of it was easy. All of it was worth the effort.

Yousif and Alia knew that to serve their Kurdish friends they would have to meet their needs at the most practical level. So they spent much of their time driving mothers to stores and helping men load machinery. They took families to appointments with doctors and helped the illiterate with government forms. They also gave out food and counseled married couples who were finding the strain of life in Kurdistan almost too much.

The Mattis gave of everything they had to help the Kurds. Not surprisingly, there came a season in which their own supplies became dangerously sparse. Conditions were worsening in Kurdistan. The economy was nearly shattered by international sanctions and the callous restrictions of Baghdad. Jobs were scarce and starvation was spreading. All of these things played on Yousif and Alia's minds.

It was during this time that an unexpected knock sounded at the Matti family's front door. When Yousif answered, he was surprised to find foreign missionaries who knew who he was. They asked if they could speak to him. It turned out that these missionaries were from Germany. Like Yousif and Alia, they had decided they wanted to make a difference for Kurdistan. With typical Germanic determination, these missionaries had raised money, flown to Turkey, purchased a truck, and filled it with food. Then, miraculously, they had driven across the border from the north. When they arrived at Duhok, they rather naively asked on the streets where the Christians were. When this question didn't quite get them what they wanted, they asked, "Where are the people who give help, like food or comfort for people in need?" Each time the answer was the same. The Mattis were "the Christians who helped people."

This is what brought these robust Germans to Yousif's door. They wanted to work with him. If he would distribute what they brought, they would begin bringing truckloads of goods right to Yousif's front door.

And so it began. The Germans—and people from other nations who also wanted to help—began unloading truckloads of goods in Yousif's front yard. One load might be filled with wheat, Vaseline, socks, and canned food. Yousif and his family would fill 15-kilogram feed bags (just over 30 pounds) with goods and pass them out from their front door. Another truckload might contain more food, but also medicine, which was like gold in the mid-1990s when a civil war raged, global sanctions choked the land, and Saddam still threatened from the south.

For years after, the Matti home served as a distribution center. People came from miles around to get help. Long lines would form at the front door of the house while the family passed out goods for hours on end. The truckloads of food and medicine that passed through the Matti home kept countless Kurds from starvation and certainly endeared the Matti family and their God to most of the people in the province of Duhok.

Not everyone was pleased. Some traditional church leaders resented these upstart evangelicals. A few mullahs were angry also. Rumors stirred that Yousif was a spy. Or perhaps he secretly worked for the Americans. Even worse, he might be in the employ of the Israelis. Didn't he often teach about Israel in his Sunday morning meetings? Didn't he call his followers to love the Jews and to pray for them? Who knows what he might be up to!

These rumors and the bitterness that the Matti generosity inspired did not make life easy for Yousif and Alia's children. At school one day, a friend ran up to Noor to tell her that her younger brother was being beaten up by some older kids. Noor ran to the commotion to find her brother, Mejid, raging at a group of larger students, his shirt torn and his face red with anger. Noor told him to leave with her. Mejid wasn't having it and turned to storm after the ones who had been picking on him. Noor finally had to drag Mejid home, all the while lecturing him that Christians didn't act this way.

These are now childhood memories that are sweet in the retelling. The truth at the time is that living as an Arab among Kurds while being accused of spying for Israel or the U.S. might easily have led to disaster. Some who worked with Yousif were killed. Rioters once broke into the Matti home and even stormed into Yousif and Alia's bedroom, a dire offense in the Muslim world. And Yousif himself was threatened on more than one occasion. When pastors and supporters began visiting from the U.S., they insisted that Yousif travel with bodyguards.

As the Kurdish civil war ended and the no-fly zone kept enemies at bay, a much better season dawned for the Matti family. Money came from Christian supporters around the world. A global network evolved that supported the Mattis in prayer and also made sure foreign governments knew who Yousif was and exerted pressure when necessary to keep him and his family safe. Kurdish churches multiplied. Kurdish politicians, judges, and Peshmerga leaders all grew to respect Yousif.

Still, Yousif seemed restless to those of us who knew him. He was delighted that hundreds of Christian Kurds were well-served by a network of churches, but he knew that this alone wouldn't change the nation as he hoped. He wanted to make a greater difference, to be involved in work that would leave Kurdistan changed even decades after Yousif was gone.

His opportunity came with a change in Kurdish educational policy. Out of a combination of Kurdish pride and Kurdish resentment of the Arabs who had caused them such terror, the Kurdish department of education determined that only Kurdish should be taught in the schools. This decision was troubling to Yousif and Alia. Not only were they Arabs who wanted their native language taught to their children, but they were by then well-traveled people who knew that Arabic—along with English, Spanish, and Chinese—was one of the great languages of commerce and technology the world over. To teach only Kurdish in the schools was to limit Kurdish influence, make Kurdistan too parochial, and to drive business and tourism from the region.

Troubled by the decision, Yousif and Alia determined to teach their children at home. This is when another turning point came. Other families wanted the Mattis to teach their children as well. It did not take long for Yousif to realize the opportunity involved. If he started a school, he could teach dozens—perhaps even hundreds and then thousands—of future leaders. He could influence their families and perhaps help shape Kurdistan for generations to come. He would have to start small, but this was the opportunity he had been looking for without even realizing it.

Yet Yousif was an engineer and not an educator. He would need help. Fortunately, that help came from Dr. George Grant, a patriarch of the classical school movement in the United States. This classical education emphasized not only reading the great books of the Western Christian canon but also teaching students to reason, to write, to debate, and to apply the truths they learned. This approach also stressed languages, art, and leadership skills. In other words, it was designed to produce learned, thinking, articulate students with a holistic worldview—just the kind of young leaders who might set the pace for a new generation.

Thus, Yousif Matti al Qas started a school. And it grew—the fruit of wise leadership and the good graces of the Kurdish regional leadership. Today, the school is just over three thousand students and is racing rapidly toward five thousand. This is astonishing progress, but size alone is not all that is revolutionary about this school. Tuition is required for each student for example. This is shocking to parents used to the free education traditionally offered in Iraq. Yet they pay the fees because of the good Yousif's school produces in the lives of their children. The school also emphasizes Western literature, something Iraqi schools have treated but rarely emphasized. This was controversial at first. Now it is welcomed, even emulated. Finally, and perhaps most revolutionary, the school prepares each student to take their classes in English. So, in the heart of Kurdistan—a region that for many years could barely keep schools running given the cost and the constant disruptions of war—there is an English language, largely Christian, Western philosophy-oriented school that is training Kurdish youth to change their world. The school is named Classical School of the Medes. Many children of the Kurdish leadership attend the school, for it is one of the great symbols of a Kurdistan that intends to invest in its young as a key to the nation's future.

And Yousif Matti al Qas is far from done with this great work. Having established a thriving high school network, now he is laying the foundation for Mede American University (MAU). Already it has eminent educators from around the world associated with it and already it has the approval and even eager endorsement of Kurdistan's leaders. They know what kind of man Yousif is. And they know when a friend has come among them who loves Kurdistan and will give his all to see her thrive. Yousif Matti al Qas is such a man.

These things are true of my friend Yousif, but there is much more and they are among the things that endear me to him. I love that he counts mullahs among his friends though he is a Christian. I love that he is loved by the Kurdish leaders, though Yousif is an Arab. I love that he has raised three wonderful children while investing in the children of Kurdistan. And I love that during the darkest days of Kurdistan's history, when devastation lay all around and death threatened, Yousif's laughter was heard. And I have seen even the chief men of Kurdistan find comfort in this man and his laugh and his unswerving love for a people who are not his own.

As long as Kurdistan has such a friend, I have no fear for Kurdistan.

EPILOGUE

THE SPIRIT
OF THE KURDS

As I write the final words of this book, Kurdistan is enduring severe birth pangs. An evil and well-armed force of Islamic extremists called ISIS—the "Islamic State of Iraq and Syria"—has cut a swath of devastation through the land of a kind seldom seen even in that country's bloody history. ISIS swarmed into villages, forced Shi'ite Muslims into the streets, and machine-gunned them to death. It forced religious minorities like the Yezidis into the mountains to starve and watch their young die of dehydration. Then, ISIS turned its ire upon Kurdistan.

It was a mistake. When ISIS confronted Iraqi troops from the south, those troops fled in fear. ISIS came to expect the same of all armed forces in Iraq. They found the Kurdish Peshmerga a different breed. The valiant stand of the Peshmerga won the attention of the world, and aid began pouring in. Then came American jets. "We cannot let the Kurds go it alone" was the chant heard in the capitals of the world. So at long last, the world came to see the valor of the Kurds and to stand as one with them.

Yet the Kurds took their stand in a manner uniquely their own. While engaged in fierce battle against extremists of their own faith, they welcomed Christian, Yezidi, and even Jewish refugees from other parts of Iraq. They helped Western aid workers leave the country and protected them until they did. Kurds from around the world sent aid and raised money from sympathetic non-Kurdish friends. All the while, KRG President Massoud Barzani tweeted about how grateful the Kurds were for the global community and how the brave Peshmerga would win the day. He seemed a digital Churchill in Kurdish garb, and it was inspiring to behold.

It will all likely prove a Kurdish version of the American Revolution, a time that tries men's souls and fashions a nation upon the anvil of adversity. It will not be the last such time, but I can think of no better epilogue to this informal tribute to the Kurds than the one they have now written for themselves through honor, skill, gratitude, and gallantry.

Only this remains to be said, then: God bless Kurdistan, and God bless the Kurds around the world.

THE WISDOM
OF THE KURDS:
100 PROVERBS

Some cultures are best understood through their arts. Others reveal themselves through their military lore. As much as the Kurds love dance, music, and art, there is an even richer understanding of their thinking to be found in the counsel of their proverbs.

Like all proverbs, these Kurdish sayings are short, practical, and pregnant with meaning. They are meant to be contemplated and to expand their meaning over time. They are the shorthand by which a people preserve what they consider wise, urge that wisdom upon each other, and pass it on in its most distilled form to the next generation.

We can almost hear these words crackling from the conversations of old women, from the scolding of the young, or as the conclusion of a tale just told among laboring men.

What we find reflected in these proverbs are a people close to nature, eager for friendship, disgusted with low character, intensely concerned about fairness, clear-eyed about the ills of the world, and reaching always for a simple brand of happiness. They have much to teach us about themselves and about wise living in our own time.

Character

If you give him cloth, he'll ask for the lining.

In a flat country, a hillock thinks itself a mountain.

It is more difficult to contend with oneself than with the world.

Thorns and roses grow on the same tree.

Everything is pardoned the brave.

Those away from the battlefield boast about their swords.

A thief not caught becomes a king.

Those who do not go to war roar like lions.

Consequence and Justice

Every sheep is hung by his own leg.

One gives twice who gives quickly.

Whoever digs a pit for his neighbor should dig it his own size.

When a bald man dies, the mourners give him curly hair
    as a present.

Destiny

No matter where you go, your destiny follows you.

Wish well, be well.

Friendship

A cup of coffee commits one to forty years of friendship.

A good companion shortens the longest road.

A thousand friends are too few; one enemy is one too many.

Better a wise foe than a foolish friend.

Eat and drink with your friends, but do not trade with them.

Of everything else the newest; of friends, the oldest.

Once a friend, always a friend.

Loneliness is a nest for the thoughts.

Deal with your friends as if they will become your enemies tomorrow, and
    deal with your enemies as if they will become your friends tomorrow.

God

Both the hunted and the hunter rely on God.

God finds a low branch for the bird that cannot fly.

If God closes one door, He opens a thousand others.

One is equally indebted to one's teacher and to God.

Hospitality

A visitor comes with ten blessings, eats one, and leaves nine.

An open door invites callers.

At table, keep a short hand; in company, keep a short tongue.

Guests bring good luck with them.

A home without guests, a village without shepherds, both are hopeless indeed.

Hunger

A hungry stomach has no ears.

Empty words will not fiil an empty stomach.

Jealousy and Property

A neighbor's hen looks as big as a goose, and his wife as young as a girl.

Better a calf of one's own than a jointly owned cow.

Kindness

A kind word warms a man through three winters.

If you wish to do a good deed, consult no one.

What you give away, you keep.

Love and the Heart

A heart in love with beauty never grows old.

See with your mind; hear with your heart.

Men and Women

A shy woman is worth a city; a shy man is worth a goat.

A woman is a fortress, a man her prisoner.

Parents

One beats one's breast who does not beat one's child.

One can never repay one's debt to one's mother.

A girl without a mother is like a mountain with no paths; a girl without a
father is like a mountain with no streams.

Patience

Patience is bitter, but it bears sweet fruit.

With patience, mulberry leaves become satin.

Trouble or Evil

A tribulation is better than a hundred warnings.

An illness comes by the pound and goes away by the ounce.

Do not roll up your trousers before reaching the stream.

Even the highest tree has an axe waiting at its foot.

Every "bad" has its "worse."

When a cat wants to eat her kittens, she says they
look like mice.

Whoever speaks evil to you of others will speak evil
of you to others.

A hundred men can sit together quietly, but when two dogs get together
there will be a fight.

Wealth and Fortune

A fool dreams of wealth, a wise man, of happiness.

A red apple invites stones.

Give nine, save ten.

God has created us brothers but has given us separate purses.

The miser and the open-handed spend the same in long run.

The rich man's wealth tires the poor man's jaw.

What is loaned goes away smiling but returns weeping.

Whoever is fond of cream should take the cow
     around with him.

With fortune on your side, you can sow salt and
     harvest grass.

Wisdom or Ignorance

A man is as wise as his head, not his years.

A wise man does his own work.

A wise man remembers his friends at all times; a fool, only when he has need
     of them.

Beauty passes; wisdom remains.

Do what your teacher says but not what he does.

Fear an ignorant man more than a lion.

For every wise man there is one still wiser.

It is easier to make a camel jump a ditch than to make a fool listen to reason.

Many will show you the way once your cart has overturned.

Study from new books but from old teachers.

To speak is to sow; to listen is to reap.

Words and the Tongue

A knife-wound heals, but a tongue-wound festers.

Kind words will unlock an iron door.

Listen a hundred times; ponder a thousand times; speak once.

Open your eyes, not your mouth.

Part with your head, but not with your secret.

Those who know do not talk; those who talk do not know.

What the heart thinks, the mouth speaks.

A threat does not lengthen your sword.

Work and Effort

A man is judged by his work.

A small key opens big doors.

Ability has no school.

Activity breeds prosperity.

Dogs bark, but the caravan goes on.

Habit is worse than rabies.

If skill could be gained by watching, every dog would become a butcher.

If you are an anvil, be patient; if you are a hammer, be strong.

It is easy to catch a serpent with someone else's hand.

It is easy to say, "Come" but difficult to say, "Go."

Stairs are climbed step by step.

Stretch your feet according to your blanket.

The devil takes a hand in what is done in haste.

Work as if you were to live forever; live as if you were to die tomorrow.

He who wants pearls has to dive into the sea.

The devil tempts all, but the idle man tempts the devil.

THE KURDS IN FILM AND FICTION

The Kurds in Film

Kurds love stories. Much like other people groups who have lived hard, isolated lives, they treasure the way stories lighten the dreary hours, interpret life and make the past of meaning to the young. The Kurds also love the storyteller's art because it is their best tool for making the world understand who they are and what they have endured. It is no wonder, then, that a younger generation of Kurds and sympathetic non-Kurds have turned to film to tell the Kurdish story.

Film is the literature of our time. While there was once a time when all educated people would understand the briefest allusion to Homer or Cicero or Dante, now our metaphors are found in popular movies. The lesson is obvious, particularly to the young: to make yourself known in our modern world, film is the stage and story is the language you must use.

The Kurds and those moved by their tale know this. It is why some of the most engaging films of our time focus upon the people of Kurdistan. If you can overcome the distraction of subtitles and resist the temptation to demand Hollywood-quality cinematography at every moment, you may discover a world that will live wondrously in your imagination all your days.

Here, then, are some of the better films about the Kurds as of the writing of this book.

1. *Salaam Dunk*
Director: David Fine
Screenwriter: David Fine
Year: 2011
Length: 78 minutes
Awards: "Best Documentary," Chicago International Film Festival; "Best Documentary Feature," Florida Film Festival 2012, Grand Jury Award, Nashville Film Festival.
Summary: The girls' basketball team at The American University of Iraq—Sulimaniya and their American coach learn about friendship, basketball, and living in a troubled land during an academic year together.

2. *1001 Apples*
Director: Taha Karimi
Screenwriter: Taha Karimi
Year: 2013
Length: 74 minutes
Awards: Best Asian Documentary, Asiatica; Best Kurdish Documentary Film, Duhok International Film Festival.

Summary: The story of Saddam Hussein's *Anfal* against the Kurds is told by a survivor who honors other survivors and their families with the gift of an apple.

3. *A Time for Drunken Horses*
Director: Bahman Ghobadi
Screenwriter: Bahman Ghobadi
Year: 2000
Length: 80 minutes
Awards: Cannes Golden Camera Award
Summary: Iranian-Kurdish children survive by smuggling along the Iran/Iraq border.

4. *Jin*
Director: Reha Erdem
Screenwriter: Reha Erdem
Year: 2013
Length: 122 minutes
Awards: Adelaide Film Festival: Best Film Award, 2013, Melbourne
International Film Festival, 2013
Summary: A 17-year old girl flees her Kurdish guerrilla unit to find solace in the wild.

5. *Son of Babylon*
Director: Mohamed Al Daradji
Screenwriter: Mohamed Al Daradji
Year: 2009
Length: 90 minutes

Awards: Berlin International Film Festival: Peace Film
Prize; British Independent Film Awards: Raindance Award;
Edinburgh International Film Festival: Honorable Mention;
Sundance Film Festival, Seattle International Film Festival:
Emerging Masters Award; all in 2010.
Summary: A boy and his determined grandmother cross Iraq in
search of a son and father lost in war.

6. *Turtles Can Fly*
Director: Bahman Ghobadi
Screenwriter: Bahman Ghobadi
Year: 2004
Length: 98 minutes
Awards: 2005 Berlin International Film Festival: Peace Film
Award; 2004 Chicago International Film Festival: Special Jury
Prize Runner-up; Rotterdam International Film Festival
Summary: On the Turkish/Iraq border, refugee children await
their fate on the eve of the U. S. invasion of Iraq.

7. *Min Dît: Children of Diyarbakir*
Director: Miraz Bezar
Screenwriter: Miraz Bezar & Evrim Alatas
Year: 2009
Length: 102 minutes
Awards: 29th International Istanbul Film Festival: Best
Director; 18th Filmfest Hamburg, 36th Ghent Film Festival:
Special Jury Prize

Summary: A Kurdish brother and sister lose their parents and are eventually forced to live on the streets of Diyarbakir, a city in eastern Turkey.

8. *Kick Off*
Director: Shawkat Amin Korki
Screenwriter: Shawkat Amin Korki
Year: 2009
Length: 81 minutes
Awards: 2009 Dubai International Film Festival: Golden Horse Awards Special mention; 2009 Pusan International Film Festival: Best Movie
Summary: Refugees from Saddam Hussein's tyrannies find shelter in a run-down stadium in the Iraqi city of Kirkuk only to discover friendship during a makeshift soccer tournament.

9. *The Herd*
Director: Zeki Ökten
Screenwriter: Yilmaz Guney
Year: 1978
Length: 114
Awards: 30th Berlin International Film Festival: Otto Dibellus Film Award; 1979 Locarno International Film Festival: Golden Leopard Award; Voted one of the ten best Turkish films by the Ankara Cinema Association.
Summary: A Turkish peasant is forced to sell his sheep in far-off Ankara due to blood feuds in his remote home village.

10. *Marooned in Iraq*
Director: Bahman Ghobadi
Screenwriter: Bahman Ghobadi
Year: 2002
Length: 97 minutes
Awards: 2002 Chicago Film Festival: Gold Plaque
Summary: A Kurdish musician takes his two sons on a journey
through Iraq in search of his lost wife.

11. *Half Moon*
Director: Bahman Ghobadi
Screenwriter: Bahman Ghobadi
Year: 2006
Length: 114 minutes
Awards: 2006 San Sebastian Film Festival: Golden Shell Award
(top prize).
Summary: The Iraqi journeys of a Kurdish musician and
his sons bring them in contact with the varying textures of
Kurdish culture.

12. *Vodka Lemon*
Director: Hiner Saleem
Screenwriter: Lei Dinety, Pauline Gouzenne
Year: 2003
Length: 90 minutes
Awards: 2003 Bangkok International Film Festival: Best Film;
Jury Award at Newport Beach Film Festival, 2003 Venice
International Film Festival: San Marco Prize

Summary: An aging man, who has only a son in remote Europe to rely upon, carves out a meaningful, poignant life in the stunning Zagros Mountains of Kurdistan.

The Kurds in Fiction

Kurdish journalists and intellectuals complain constantly about the meager state of Kurdish fiction. It is easy to feel their frustration, but the problem is not in a lack of material. It is in the small number of publishers willing to champion Kurdish-themed books, in the lack of translations of Kurdish writing, and in a biased international publishing industry.

Though there are many novels that could be and ought to be listed in this brief list of Kurdish-themed novels, it serves little purpose to list books not available in English or on Amazon.com. We should hope that digital publishing and more enlightened attitudes will help remove some of the barriers to a long-awaited Kurdish literary renaissance. Until that day arrives, the following are some of the most helpful novels about the Kurds that are readily available in English.

1. *A Fire in My Heart: Kurdish Tales* by Diane Edgecomb
Every culture has its stories. In fact, cultures are largely created by stories. The Kurdish culture is no different. This collection of thirty fairy tales reveals more of who the Kurds are than most histories. From a uniquely Kurdish version of Cinderella to the Kurdish Hercules—Resteme' Zal—these are the tales that have helped to keep Kurdish identity alive for generations.

2. *Five Sisters: A Modern Novel of Kurdish Women* by Kit
Anderson
Written by a teacher with extensive experience among the
Kurds, this tender novel is built upon the genuine stories of
heroic Kurdish women.

3. *Honor: A Novel* by Elif Shafak
A powerful exploration of Kurdish culture as it survives outside
of Kurdistan, this novel is by an award-winning writer who
is also the most-read woman novelist in Turkey. The London
Times called *Honor* a "stunning novel...exotic, evocative, and
utterly gripping."

4. *The Word Not Spoken* by Laurie Fraser
This first novel by Fraser, an award-winning poet, reveals an
admittedly Western perspective on the Kurdish and Turkish
cultures. The narrative captures fascinating yet sometimes
inexplicable details of Kurdish beliefs and daily life.

5. *The Lost Word* by Oya Baydar
The plight of the Kurds in modern Turkey is the theme of this
popular Turkish novel only recently translated into English.
Part political thriller, part psychological drama, and part
textured love story, this novel by a world-renowned author is
finely woven and historically accurate.

A WORD ABOUT CHRISTOPHER HITCHENS

I never feel quite as divided of heart as I do when remembering Christopher Hitchens. I loved him for his wit, his learning, his courage, his humor, and his unfashionable patriotism. I loved him, too, for his costly devotion to the Kurds. When I saw him on a cable news program wearing a Kurdish flag lapel pin and extolling the Kurds—*my* Kurds—as heroic people, I thought I had never seen such a man.

Yet he despised the religion I've staked my life upon and never sidestepped an opportunity to urinate upon what I hold dear. He celebrated the deaths of men who were fathers to me and once suggested suicide as the only remedy for people of my religious "malady." After digesting one too many of his rants against Christianity, I began referring to him simply as "The Antichrist."

He would have taken it as a compliment, had he even noticed. He barely knew who I was. We met in a green room at MSNBC in New York where I was to appear on *Topic A with Tina Brown* with Paul Krugman and he was pre-recording an interview for another show. We shared pleasantries for a few minutes before he asked me about the topic of my interview. I told him that Krugman and I would be talking about the influence of religion on the Bush administration. My book *The Faith of George W. Bush* was on the bestseller lists at the time. He knew of it but had not read it. He had no intention of reading it, he said. Religion was what he most despised about Bush and his ilk.

And so it began. The next five minutes were among the least civil of any I've known. Mercifully, a producer interrupted us to summon me to the set. I rose to shake Hitchens' hand. He remained seated, shook my hand, and said, "Well, at least you've not been lobotomized." I think he meant that I was not as stupid as most of the stupid people in my stupid faith.

What I wish is that we had met at a later time when we might have joined forces in behalf of the Kurds. I admired his tireless championing of their cause and would have happily stood with him. He knew nothing of my history with the Kurds. Perhaps he would not have cared, but I think he was the kind of man who would have welcomed aid from any source in support of a noble cause. The Kurds are just that and no one knew it as well as Christopher Hitchens.

I have chosen to begin each chapter in this book with his words. It is my way of honoring the part of him that I can honor and, hopefully, of reminding us all that Christopher Hitchens the anti-religion bigot was the same Christopher Hitchens who risked his life to travel Kurdistan and then risked his career to explain Kurdistan to the world.

He could be both a bully and a bore, but he evidenced a greater moral clarity and sense of honor than most of the guardians of morality and honor I have met. He wrote fearlessly, as in the sentiments below about international affairs, and only the small and the desiccated would refuse to esteem him for it.

Sooner or later the Saddam Hussein regime will fall, either of its own weight or from the physical and mental collapse of its leader or from endogenous or exogenous pressure. On that day one will want to be able to look the Iraqi and Kurdish people in the eye and say that we thought seriously about their interest and appreciated that, because of previous interventions that were actually in Saddam's favor, we owed them a debt. It's this dimension that seems to me lacking in the current antiwar critique.

ACKNOWLEDGMENTS

The story of the Kurds can be complex. Even my largely personal remembrances in these pages required the help of experts to set context and explain meaning.

I am indebted to my long-time mentor, Dr. George Grant, for access to his journals and insightful research in the field of Middle East studies. General George Sada honored me with his valuable time on an icy cold day in Tulsa. I am forever grateful. Yousif Matti al Qas and his daughter, Noor, offered invaluable perspective not only upon their own story but also upon the recent history of the Kurds. David Dillard, president of Servant Group International, allowed me to interview him, made connections for me, and touched me with his devotion to the Kurds. Jim Dausch and Dan Williamson granted me not only the benefits of their literary gifts but also of their business experience in the Middle East and their knowledge of military affairs.

Belmont University in Nashville graciously allowed my daughter, Elizabeth Mansfield, to do her senior internship with our firm during the creation of this book. Elizabeth edited, attended interviews, organized photographs, and gave wise counsel. I am proud of her beyond expressing and will always be grateful for her imprint upon these pages. She grew up hearing of the Kurds and having more than a few of them in her home. I'm not sure she fully understood who they were until she began working on this book. She underwent, then, both a journey into Kurdistan and a journey into her own past. I'm thankful to have been at her side while she did.

There were many in Kurdistan who labored to help. Some wrote out their remembrances, some visited with me via Skype, and some sat with me during my recent trips to Iraq. Among these were the Honorable Moshin Dizayee, the Honorable Khalid Jamal Alber, General Director of Christian Affairs, the Honorable Xeri Bozani, the Honorable Dr. Azad M. A. Naqshbandi of the University of Salahaddin, the Honorable Sadi Ahmed Pire, Dr. Saadi Al-Malih, General Director of Syriac Culture and Art, eminent journalist Salaam Abdullah of KHABAT, and the Honorable Aram Ahmed Muhammad of the Ministry of Martyrs and *Anfal* Affairs. Also immensely helpful were Zino Mustafa, CEO of Rasan Pharmaceuticals in

Sulimaniya, and Aveen Hawrami, Director of the American International School of Kurdistan in Erbil.

Tamara Quinn, head of AIX Global, and one of the most amazing women and Iraqis I've ever met, wisely guided me in my work. Her Director of Business Development, Raz Rasool, was wonderfully knowledgeable and eager to help in securing interviews. My deep gratitude to both of these stirring champions of their people.

There are many Kurdish friends I cannot name but whose stories are told in these pages. They fled Saddam, fought his troops, held the dying, buried their dead, lived as strangers in a strange land, opened their homes and hearts to foreigners like me, and rebuilt their lives in the unfamiliar world of America and, sometimes, in the unfamiliar world of their own changing homeland. I honor them as heroes. They have honored me with their friendship and their stories.

Finally, I recall the day a Kurdish friend sat with me at a teashop in Istanbul. Our conversation turned to wives. He had three and wondered if I knew. "Yes," I said. "I know your religion and your history. I know you have three wives." A few moments of thoughtful silence went by. "And what do you think of this?" he asked. We had come to a playful friendship and I decided to lean into it. "I think you may have three times more trouble than I do!" We laughed together and then he said, "No, perhaps it is that your one wife is worth many."

He was right. My one wife, Beverly—friend, lover, partner, agent, editor, and final judge of all I write—is indeed worth many.

A SELECT
BIBLIOGRAPHY

Bird, Christiane. *A Thousand Sighs, A Thousand Revolts: Journeys in Kurdistan*. New York: Random House, 2005.

Bremer III, L. Paul. *My Year in Iraq*. New York: Simon and Schuster Threshold Editions, 2006.

Caban, Dana. *Kurds: A Nation Frozen in Time*. Bloomington: AuthorHouse, 2009.

Cottee, Simon and Thomas Cushman, eds. *Christopher Hitchens and His Critics: Terror, Iraq, and the Left*. New York: New York University Press, 2008.

Grant, George. *The Blood of the Moon: Understanding the Historic Struggle Between Islam and Western Civilization*. Nashville: Thomas Nelson, Inc., 2008.

Gunter, Michael M. *The A to Z of the Kurds*. Lanham: The Scarecrow Press, Inc., 2009.

Hitchens, Christopher. *Hitch-22: A Memoir*. New York: Grand Central Publishing, 2010.

Howell, Georgina. *Gertrude Bell: Queen of the Desert, Shaper of Nations*. New York: Farrar, Straus and Giroux, 2007.

Hussein, Fuad, ed. *International Conference on Genocide Against the Kurdish People: Documenting the Genocide Against the Kurds* (Serial No. 03). Erbil: Aras Press, 2008.

Izady, Mehrdad R. *The Kurds: A Concise Handbook.* Washington, DC: Taylor and Francis, Inc., 1992.

Lawrence, Quil. *Invisible Nation: How the Kurds' Quest for Statehood Is Shaping Iraq and the Middle East.* New York: Walker & Company, 2008.

Lawrence, T. E. *The Seven Pillars of Wisdom.* Garden City: Doubleday, Doran & Company, 1935.

McDowall, David. *A Modern History of the Kurds.* New York: I. B. Tauris & Co, Ltd, 1996.

Meiselas, Susan. *Kurdistan: In the Shadow of History.* New York: Random House, 1997.

Nasar, Vali. *The Shia Revival: How Conflicts within Islam Will Shape the Future.* New York: W. W. Norton & Company, 2007.

Sada, Georges, with Jim Nelson Black. *Saddam's Secrets: How an Iraqi General Defied and Survived Saddam Hussein.* Nashville, TN: Thomas Nelson Publishers, 2006.

Sheil, Mary Leonora Woulfe and Justin Sheil. *Glimpses of Life and Manners in Persia.* London: J. Murray, 1856.

NOTES

Chapter 1

1. Christopher Hitchens, "Iraq: Worth the Price," *Washington Post* (March 11, 2008). Also, see "A Word About Christopher Hitchens" in the back matter of this book.

Chapter 2

1. Hitchens, "Goodbye to All That," *Harper's* (November 1998).

Chapter 3

1. Hitchens, "The Struggle of the Kurds," *National Geographic* (August 1992).

Chapter 4

1. Hitchens, "The Struggle of the Kurds."
2. Larry Collins and Dominique Lapierre, *O Jerusalem!* (New York: Simon & Schuster, 1972), 83.
3. Genesis 10:10 KJV.
4. David McDowall, *A Modern History of the Kurds* (New York: I. B. Taurus, 1996), 3.
5. Cigerxwin was a pen name. The poet's original name was Sheikhmous Hasan.
6. Acts 2:9 KJV
7. Mehrdad R. Izady, *The Kurds: A Concise Handbook* (Bristol: Taylor & Francis, 1992), 49.
8. Ibid., 55.
9. Ibid., 59.

Chapter 5

1. Hitchens, *Love, Poverty, and War: Journeys and Essays* (New York: Nation Books, 2004), 357.

2. Ralph S. Solecki, *Shanidar: The First Flower People* (New York: Knopf, 1971).
3. Izady, 238.
4. Ibid.
5. Ibid.
6. George Grant, *The Last Crusader: The Untold Story of Christopher Columbus* (Wheaton, IL: Crossway Books, 1992), 66.
7. Jonathan Edwards, *The Works of Jonathan Edwards* (Edinburgh: The Banner of Truth Trust, 1979), 607.
8. This matter of "Arabization" is of great concern not only to the Kurds but to many ethnic groups that wish to embrace Islam but also retain their ethnic identity. In Islam, the official language is Arabic, pilgrimage must be made to an Arab country, prayer is offered while facing an Arab city, and Arab customs and thought-forms prevail. It can mean that a people like the Kurds are asked to surrender their culture in order to embrace their religion, that their faith comes with what amounts to an ethnic takeover.

Chapter 6

1. Thomas Cushman and Simon Cottee, eds., *Christopher Hitchens and His Critics* (New York: NYU Press, 2008), 101.
2. Hitchens, *Hitch-22: A Memoir of Christopher Hitchens* (New York: Hachette Book Group, 2010), 296.
3. Al Hurriya, *From Nebuchadnezzar to Saddam Hussein: Babylon Rises Again*, 4th ed. (Baghdad: Iraqi Ministry of Information and Culture, 1987, 1990), 7.

Chapter 7

1. Hitchens, *Love, Poverty, and War*, 356.
2. Middle East Watch, *Genocide in Iraq*, 106.
3. Susan Meiselas, *Kurdistan: In the Shadow of History* (New York: Random House, 1997), 315.
4. Ibid., 317.
5. Hitchens, *Love, Poverty, and War*, 357.

Chapter 8

1. Hitchens, *Hitch-22*, 297–298.
2. Lawrence, *Invisible Nation*, 39.
3. Turkish Probe, vol. 1, no. 3 (December 1992).

4. George H. W. Bush and Brent Scowcroft, *A World Transformed* (New York: Knopf, 1998), 472.
5. Lawrence, *Invisible Nation*, 45.
6. Quoted in David McDowall, *A Modern History of the Kurds* (New York: I. B. Tauris, 1996), 371.
7. Ibid.
8. Rafet Balli of *Milliyet*, in *The Independent* (April 23, 1991).
9. *International Herald Tribune* (March 30, 1991).
10. *The Independent* (April 11, 1991).
11. *The Independent* (April 7, 1991).
12. Adolph Hitler was baptized as a Roman Catholic when he was an infant, but he later renounced his Catholicism. He used Christian language in his speeches and twisted Christian doctrines to feed anti-Semitism among the German people and to cover the perversions of the Nazi regime. For further study of this topic, consult *The Rise and Fall of the Third Reich* by William Shirer.

Chapter 9
1. Hitchens, *Hitch-22*, 339–340.

ABOUT THE AUTHOR

Stephen Mansfield is a New York Times best-selling author whose works include *The Faith of George W. Bush, The Search for God and Guinness, Never Give In: The Extraordinary Character of Winston Churchill, The Faith of Barack Obama, Lincoln's Battle With God,* and *Mansfield's Book of Manly Men.* He is a popular speaker who coaches and advises leaders worldwide. Mansfield lives in Nashville and Washington, DC, with his wife, Beverly, who is an award-winning songwriter and producer. For further information, log onto StephenMansfield.TV.

WORTHY
PUBLISHING

If you enjoyed this book, will you consider sharing the message with others?

- Mention the book in a Facebook post, Twitter update, Pinterest pin, blog post, or upload a picture through Instagram.

- Recommend this book to those in your small group, book club, workplace, and classes.

- Head over to facebook.com/worthypublishing or facebook.com/MansfieldWrites, "LIKE" the page, and post a comment as to what you enjoyed the most.

- Tweet "I recommend reading #MiracleOfTheKurds by @MansfieldWrites // @worthypub"

- Pick up a copy for someone you know who would be challenged and encouraged by this message.

- Write a book review online.

You can subscribe to Worthy Publishing's newsletter at worthypublishing.com.

WORTHY PUBLISHING
FACEBOOK PAGE

WORTHY PUBLISHING
WEBSITE